WATCH IT COME DOWN

Human Consciousness, Astrology, and the Death and Rebirth of America

GREGORY PAUL MARTIN

ISBN-13: 978-1-79-504316-8

DEDICATION

This book is dedicated to the memory of John F. Kennedy, the most courageous, compassionate, eloquent President in the history of the United States of America – a man of peace. And to Jane Roberts, the primary source of the wisdom of the ages birthing the most profound paradigm shift in consciousness in human history, *The Cosmocentric Revolution*.

CONTENTS

ACKNOWLEDGMENTS

This book would not have been possible without the tireless energy, love and support of my beautiful wife, Cherie Rose Martin.

"When you get into a tight place and everything goes against you, till it seems as though you could not hold on a minute longer, never give up then, for that is just the place and time that the tide will turn. When you're down to nothing, God is up to something. The faithful see the invisible, believe the incredible, and receive the impossible. Where liberty dwells, there is my country."

Benjamin Franklin

"The purpose of a writer is to keep civilization from destroying itself."

Albert Camus

"In order to rise from its own ashes, a phoenix first must burn."

Octavia Butler, *Parable of the Talents*

"The true power is in the human imagination, which dares to speculate on that which is not yet, but that can be."

Jane Roberts, *The Nature of Personal Reality*

INTRODUCTION

The mighty little book you hold in your hands is the most important book on human consciousness, astrology, and the future of America and the rest of the world you will ever read. If you understand and embrace its message, acting on it with every ounce of your soul, with every fiber of your being, you will assume your God-given role in the most revolutionary paradigm shift in human history, a transformation in our understanding of the nature of reality, the universe and our place within it more profound and monumental than the Copernican Revolution -- the revelation that the earth revolves around the Sun that shattered the mistaken model of the universe with the earth at its center conceived by Plato and Aristotle, cemented five hundred years later by the man lionized as the leading authority on astrology in the ancient world, the Greek-Alexandrian polymath, Ptolemy.

Massive transformational energy – the most revolutionary upgrade in consciousness humanity has ever experienced -- is with us, right here, right now. That is why the shadowy puppet masters pulling the strings behind the White House – big oil, the military-industrial complex, the Conservative Christian evangelical movement – are so intent on keeping you in confusion, distraction and fear. That is why America feels so fragile, desperate and dark. The darkness is being exposed and is relentlessly pushing back, resisting the inevitable oncoming of the light. It is always darkest before the dawn, and that darkness holds truths more precious than your wildest dreams if you can find the courage to shine your light on them. That is what is being asked of you now.

A brave, bold, new understanding of freedom and power – the limitless power of divine human consciousness – is sweeping us up in its almighty grasp. We are the creators of our own reality. Now and forever. The awesome

3

power of your human mind is all. There are no rules. Nothing is holding you back. There never was, and there never will be. You are the master of your world, the captain of your fate. No matter what circumstances you were born into, you were born in a state of grace and shall remain in that state of grace forever, total power and dominion at your fingertips. Your future is a blank slate. Nothing is written, except your birth and death. Every possible future exists in the vast field of infinite probabilities and if you believe it, expect it and desire it with a fierce, passionate intensity, so that you can see it, hear it, smell it, taste it, touch it and feel it, you can access and live your highest probable future right now, with a snap of your fingers, in the literal blink of an eye.

The focus and intensity of your beliefs, expectations, passion and desire is all.

Embracing and living the maximum individual expression of the divine power of God, the joy and light within you, is your only true purpose. That is why you are here. That is why you are alive on earth today. Unless you insist on remaining unconscious, everything else - every outmoded, archaic law of astrology included – is a lie.

Much has been written on the subject of astrology, a lot of it repetitive, regurgitated mumbo jumbo, meaningless guff, the majority of astrologers still in thrall to their egos, hidebound by tradition and the past and thus incapable of providing any powerful, original insight into the astonishing discoveries about the nature of the universe and human reality being unveiled to us now. Their knowledge gleaned from books they have read, other astrologers they have studied with who have read the same books, or courses they have found in colleges or online their level of understanding is woefully inadequate.

Astrology is an ancient belief system, not reality. And like any belief system it is limited. The startling new vision of human consciousness and the universe shaking the foundations of our world right now will knock down every antiquated pillar in astrology's antediluvian bag of tricks like pins in a bowling alley in the same way it will turn our comprehension of who and what we are and our understanding of the nature of the cosmos and the power of the human mind upside down and inside out.

You stand at the very center of that revolution, because the vital missing piece has been human consciousness itself – the literally limitless, awesome power of the human mind.

At its most fundamental level your astrological chart is a map of your

4

soul's psychology in this lifetime, the challenging energies in the chart depicting your unconscious belief system.

It is not a prison.

In the words of the founder of analytical psychology, Carl Gustav Jung, another polymath genius who studied the stars using the information in his patients' charts to help him effect their cures, "Until you make the unconscious conscious, it will direct your life, and you will call it fate."

"The fault, dear Brutus, is not in our stars, but in ourselves that we are underlings", wrote Shakespeare in *Julius Caesar*. Beliefs are not reality. Your thoughts, expectations and beliefs **create** reality. Change your mind and you will change your world. There is no such thing as preordained destiny. There is no 'out there' out there. Nothing is written. Instead, your existence and future are couched in a vast sea of limitless probabilities. Every fully conscious, self-realized man or woman knows this and if they have committed to living this truth they have reclaimed their free will, de facto becoming miracle workers, their blocks to spiritual sight, the challenging energies in their charts, no longer affecting them, because they have transcended them. Like Jesus, or any other spiritual master, they have stepped outside of time.

Although their egos argue ceaselessly to the contrary, spiritual Neanderthals like Trump, his family and his tribe of criminal confreres in the darkest, most corrupt incarnation of the Republican party in history have no free will whatsoever, because they have done everything to avoid their spiritual journeys in this lifetime, determined to remain unconscious, and thus possess a very limited understanding of who and what they are and the astonishing, transcendent powers of the human mind. It is because of this Trump now finds himself facing the ineluctable, devastating blowback from a lifetime of duplicity, malignance and crime that, beginning with the Super Blood Wolf Moon total eclipse of January 21, 2019 will slowly be unleashed on him in a sequence of shocking, scandalous events that will make Nixon's downfall over Watergate look like an innocent Sunday school picnic outing in the park.

Because he has refused to come to consciousness and evolve, between now and the end of 2021 Trump will go down like a $20 hooker.

That is written. *That is* a fait accompli.

Nations, like individuals, have astrology charts too, the map drawn for the date and time of the nation's birth, as with any individual the chart describing the nation's psychology, the drives and gifts of its soul, the blocks to spiritual sight the nation has incarnated to transcend, as well as its highest potential destiny.

Because a nation is made up of millions of people, all of whom are at different stages of their psychological evolution, unless a country is rooted in a profound, ancient spiritual tradition – such as Bali, or Tibet -- as with any unconscious individual the nation is being run by its collective ego and in the same way has no free will, the nation's future unfolding precisely as it is written in its chart, appearing to the rest of the world as that nation's 'fate'. That is why, as in the case of Trump, America has no choice but to undergo the profound experience of death and rebirth we are witnessing beginning to unfold now.

From 2018 to 2023, for the first time in America's history Pluto, lord of death and rebirth, corruption and purification, the darkness and the light, makes its slow, protracted return to the exact degree of the zodiac it stood at on the day of the nation's birth, July 4, 1776, the date of the publication of *The Declaration of Independence*, relentlessly exposing every ounce of depravity, immorality and corruption the nation has descended into in the two and half centuries since America was born that continues to exist today, unabated, in almost every aspect of American life, particularly those areas ruled by the sign of Capricorn – big business, big oil, multi-national corporations, Wall Street and the government.

Pluto is a fierce, intense, unrelenting energy that takes no prisoners, its function to ruthlessly expose and destroy every last vestige of corrupt, defiled energy in an individual, nation, or organization, rebuilding it at a higher level. The return of Pluto to its exact position in the nation's chart for the first time in America's history is the astrological symbol of the nation's death and rebirth.

Things are too far gone. For more than a hundred years the skullduggery and iniquity have run too deep. The so called leader of the free world has run amok, straying a million miles from its intended destiny. Just like Islam, America has been high-jacked, leading the world to the edge of a calamitous, precipitous cliff, the verge of self-destruction. The nation has lost the plot. It's time for the whole rotten, decaying, dying, filthy system to come crashing pell-mell to the ground.

If in the dark days to come you find yourself falling into fear at the chaos you see erupting around you, if you begin to lose hope as you witness the old, corrupt, dying America falling apart before your very eyes, remember this. You have not been wrong. You have simply come early to the party.

If you screw your courage to the sticking place, using the deeply challenging energies of this time to own who and what you are, the awesome power and responsibility of your God-given mind, plumbing the depths of your hitherto unacknowledged, limitless power, consciously, passionately altering your future, on the far side of this experience you will find yourself living in an America and a world that have been magically changed forever.

America and the world will have been reborn.

Completed in Paris in January, 2019 -- the City of Light, the city that gave birth to the political, philosophical and cultural revolution that inspired Thomas Jefferson, Benjamin Franklin and John Adams in their drafting of *The Declaration of Independence*, that designed and built *La Liberté éclairante le monde* -- the Statue of Liberty — a gift to the American people from the French celebrating the birth of a nation that was to stand as a beacon of light and hope for the world, mirroring the principles of liberty, equality and brotherhood upon which the French revolution was founded, *Watch It Come Down* was begun on a road trip across America in the late summer and fall of 2018 as I witnessed the fragmentation, violence and rage erupting in almost every walk of American in the destructive wake of the Kavanaugh hearings.

To an outsider, an Englishman with an American wife who has spent a large part of his life in the United States in love with the beauty and integrity of the Founding Fathers' vision it was a distressing experience and continues to be so. There is no doubt about it. America has plunged into the terrifying night sea journey prefigured in the nation's astrological chart. This is the long, bleak, dark night of Lady Liberty's deeply-troubled soul.

While on the level of form it is heartbreaking to watch, what is crucial to understand is that this process of death and rebirth is built into the nation's destiny and is in fact vital to America's future prosperity and health. Without death there can come no new life. To rise from its own ashes, a phoenix first must burn. And above all else, in terms of politics and the elevation of a mendacious, malignant psychopath named Donald J. Trump to the office of Chief Executive of the United States of America, in the coming months as you witness his shocking, inevitable, ignominious fall and the whole rotten, decaying system come tumbling to the ground you should give a universal shout of thanks that at long last you have no choice but to open up your eyes and witness the brutal, ugly, God's honest truth.

Big daddy – your elected emperor in Washington -- has no clothes. And no matter what your opinion of Barack Obama, except for one brief, shining moment when President John F. Kennedy sat behind the Resolute desk inside the Oval Office in the early 1960s, in modern times he never has.

It is critical you ask yourself the following question – why are you alive at this time? Why you? Why now, at this, the most pivotal moment in human history? Why have you chosen to be here to witness the death and rebirth of America and the salvation of the world?

The answer is you have chosen to be here to save the planet and to wake yourself up to who and what you truly are, to claim and express the awesome, limitless power of your human mind. You are the answer, the risen Christ, the most powerful force in the universe. You are the light of the world. There is no 'out there' out there. The universe is a hologram. Your mind creates the future and can turn it back to full creation in an instant.

Hidden within every calamity we privately or collectively experience is an invisible gift forcing us to embrace powers of the human psyche we have hitherto ignored, or unconsciously been afraid of. Within every so called catastrophe, each apparent disaster is a secret blessing designed to lead us -- if we keep our egos in check and pay attention to what our inner teacher is trying to tell us – to a critical turning point, a heretofore unseen road that, if followed, will lead us to a bright and brilliant, brand new day.

This truth is as true for each and every one of us in the course of our individual rights of passage as it is with the profound experience of death and rebirth America finds itself grappling with as a nation today. This is the truth the universe is calling you to embrace and live now.

While on the surface what appears to be, and shall continue to appear to be a monumental disaster – the literal destruction of America from the inside out – it is vital you realize that on a deeper level what is happening is that the highest part of you is attempting to break through your mental fog, blindness and confusion to wake you up to the phenomenal power lying dormant within you -- and that as everyone who reads this book who has experienced any kind of deep spiritual work will understand, far from being the end, death is merely a change of form – that as with any individual, from this experience of death America will bring forth a new life.

Your job is to keep your eyes on the prize, refusing to buy into the fear-mongering and confusion that will inevitably be created and perpetrated by the media and those wishing to save themselves in Washington as the whole vulgar, shoddy Trump Presidential freak show comes crashing to the ground.

A clarion call to every man, woman and child who still believes in the fundamental principles on which America was founded, this book asks its readers to address the following most critically important questions of our time.

What was the original vision of America conceived by the Founding Fathers?

How far has America strayed from that vision?

How deeply do you care about the fate of the planet?

Do you have free will? Does life happen _to_ you? Or are you the creator of your own reality?

Do your thoughts, expectations, and beliefs influence the nature and outcome of your experiences and of mass events?

Are you a victim? Or are you 100% responsible for what occurs in your life and what you see in the world around you?

Do you want your children to live, or to die?

The next five years are going to be the most challenging in America's history. And you are living here and now for a reason.

You have a choice. You can bury your head in the sand and continue to live on the timeline in which America and its war machine drives the entire human race off the cliff of our collective oblivion. Or you can open your eyes and look at the corruption, cowardice and duplicity, and in several cases the naked, cold-blooded evil staring back at you from faces of men and women who for too many years have been blindly elected into office in Washington – change your probable future, and take back the power.

Which you? Which America? Which world?

The red pill, or the blue pill?

The choice is yours.

"Turning and turning in the widening gyre,
The falcon cannot hear the falconer,
Things fall apart; the center cannot hold;
Mere anarchy is loosed upon the world,
The blood-dimmed tide is loosed, and everywhere
The ceremony of innocence is drowned;
The best lack all conviction, while the worst
Are full of passionate intensity."

W.B. Yeats, *The Second Coming*

"The dark night of the soul comes just before revelation. When everything is lost and all seems darkness comes the new life, and all that is needed."

Joseph Campbell

"What the caterpillar calls the end of the world, the master calls a butterfly"

Richard Bach, *Illusions: The Adventures of a Reluctant Messiah*

1 APOCALYPSE NOW

You and I are living at the most critical moment in human history, a time when, because of our collective indolence and naivety, we are being forced into a rude and brutal awakening.

We are being forced to wake up and smell the coffee.

The smell is not good. The coffee is burnt and stale. The diner we are sitting in is tired and sad. Swarms of woodlice are teeming from the pockmarked crevices in the rotting wooden walls. Bloated, fattened, self-serving cockroaches are crawling across the cracked, broken, dusty, old table tops, devouring every crumb of nourishment in sight. We are a billion miles from the utopian dreams of brotherhood, equality, peace and love of the '60s. It does not feel good. It feels lousy. It feels as if we are lost. It feels like America is finished. It feels as if the whole world is going to hell in a hand basket.

We are not lost. America is not finished. The world is not going to hell in a hand basket. Not yet. But if you and I don't wake up – right now – owning our God-given responsibility and power, vehemently asserting our rights as citizens of the world and shepherds of the earth, relentlessly shining our light, taking action however we are guided, in whatever way the Holy Spirit moves us, within less than thirty years such an apocalyptic vision of the future – a future in which there will no longer be a United States of America, nor any of the rest of the world – will become our inevitable reality.

How does that make you feel?

I pray to God it makes you wake up. For that at its most fundamental

11

level is the profound purpose of this book.

My intention is not to scare you. My intention is precisely the opposite. My intention is to provoke you, inspire you, incite and uplift you. Above all else my intention is to wake you up and show you how to take back the power. Because if that doesn't happen none of us on this Godforsaken planet are going to make it. Yet before that can happen we must together take a long, hard look at exactly what is happening in America and the world today.

The dark future timeline I have described above is the one we are currently collectively living on, all this talk of probable cataclysmic global gloom and doom bruising the human horizon unfortunately no fantasy. I am writing these words on Christmas Eve, 2018. The celebration of the birth of joy, love, light and peace into the world.

Consider this.

Three weeks ago America, the third largest oil producing nation in the world, joined Russia and Saudi Arabia, the world's two leading producers, in a joint refusal to endorse the findings of a critical report delivered at COP24, the United Nations Climate Change Conference in Poland, on the earth's now deadly ominous levels of global warming, a desperate attempt to avert an environmental disaster of cataclysmic proportions that scientists have predicted will inevitably occur should we fail to reverse the levels of carbon dioxide in the earth's atmosphere by at least 45% by 2030.

Two weeks prior to COP24 it was reported deforestation in the Brazilian Amazon has risen to its highest level in a decade, 7,900 square kilometers of the rainforest felled in the last twelve months, a rise of 14% since the same time least year, an area bigger than the size of Manhattan lost between August and October alone, the prospect of victory for Brazil's Donald Trump, the right-wing populist Presidential candidate, Jair Bolsonaro, whose strongest election vow was to open up the rainforest for strip mining, farming and dam building, building a freeway through the Amazon while withdrawing Brazil from the Paris Climate Accord emboldening illegal actions by Brazilian logging companies. Bolsonaro has since been elected, hours after taking office making good on his promise, launching a full-frontal assault on the environmental protections of the Amazon.

The Amazon rainforest is the largest tropical rainforest in the world, deforestation the second-largest contributor to climate change after the burning of fossil fuels, accounting for an estimated 10% of greenhouse gas emissions, adding more carbon dioxide to the atmosphere than the total number of cars and trucks on the world's roads. Rainforests are literally the lungs of the planet. Left intact they act like sponges, soaking up carbon dioxide in the atmosphere converting it into plant material. When a rainforest is cut down or burned it releases the large amounts of carbon dioxide stored in the trees, reversing those positive effects.

This combination of the wealthiest, most powerful nation in the world and the third largest producer of oil rallying behind the number one and two producers, Russia and Saudi Arabia, in a refusal to ratify an attempt to address the most critical environmental issue in history together with the newly elected President of Brazil opening up the Amazon rainforest for wholesale exploitation and pillage is the most ominous confluence of events in terms of the prospects of the future survival of humanity and the planet imaginable.

On the same day Trump's EPA representatives presented their insane, indefensible argument for rolling back environmental regulations in America at COP24, actively promoting the nation's continued dependence on coal and other dirty fossil fuels, a United Nations report was issued announcing the earth's oceans are warming twice as fast as previously believed, Antarctica losing six times more ice annually than it was forty years ago, the NOAA's annual Arctic Report Card simultaneously confirming 2018 was the second warmest year on record, surface air temperatures in the Arctic warming twice as fast as the rest of the globe, an unprecedented change scientists have deemed responsible for the severe weather conditions all around the world, the extreme winter storms in the eastern United States included.

The NOAA report concluded with the tragic news polar bear, caribou, and wild reindeer populations have declined by more than 56% over the past two decades, and that contamination of sea ice by microplastics has been found at far higher concentrations in the Arctic ocean than in the majority of global waters, the micro-sized particles consumed by sea birds and marine life leading to accumulations in higher-level organisms -- i.e. humans.

Microplastic contamination at these alarming levels has also been found in the deepest parts of the Mariana Trench, 36,000 feet below the surface of the Pacific, as many as 2,000 pieces of microplastic per a single liter of water. This ominous spread of microplastic pollution in our oceans stems from five enormous areas of accumulated ocean plastic, the largest of which, the Great Pacific Garbage Patch located between the coast of California and Hawaii, now covers an area three times the size of Texas.

The situation with regard to this additional environmental ticking time bomb of potentially apocalyptic proportions is no better than that of global warming. While five of the world's leading industrial powers signed the G7 Oceans Plastics Charter in 2018 pledging to increase plastic recycling by 50%, working towards 100% recyclable plastics by 2030, not a single government in the world has as thus far so much as lifted a finger to tackle the enormous environmental threat posed by the five areas of the world's oceans awash in plastic, the only attempt currently undertaken to tackle the Great Pacific Garbage Patch funded by a private non-profit organization based in Europe, *Ocean Clean Up*.

A recent U. N. environmental report concluded that unless concerted action is taken by humanity by 2050 there will be more plastic in the world's oceans than fish.

With regard to the decimation of global wildlife the signs indicating how close we are to total self-destruction are similarly terrifying, the earth currently losing its biodiversity at a rate that in the past has only been seen during periods of mass extinctions. In October, 2018 a Worldwide Wildlife Fund report concluded that because of human-driven changes – overexploitation of wildlife, pollution, habitat loss and degradation – worldwide species counts have been reduced by a staggering 60% over the last four decades, a statistic that together with the threat posed by global warming and the possibility of the outbreak of nuclear war driven by North Korea's nuclear program, tensions between America and Russia, and between America and China in the South China Sea, the buildup of nuclear arsenals in Pakistan and India, and Trump pulling America out of the Iran deal has prompted The Bulletin of the Atomic Scientists to advance the hands of the Doomsday Clock – the symbol measuring how close mankind is to the likelihood of self-destruction -- to two minutes to midnight for the first time since 1953, the height of the cold war.

According to every esteemed scientific body in the world – the U.N. Intergovernmental Panel on Climate Change, the Convention on Biological Diversity, the U.S. National Academy of Sciences, the National Resources Defense Council, the Global Environmental Facility, the Global Education Project, the Union of Concerned Scientists, and individuals of the rank of Ellen Stofan, the former chief scientist and Head of NASA –- the verdict on the environment is in, and now indisputable, cold, hard scientific fact – fact that, thanks to the myopic, self-serving leadership we have thus far foolishly collectively entrusted to steer the course of this planet's fragile ship barely makes it to the front pages of the newsfeed of whichever cell phone service you use, winding up buried beneath the endless swill of fear-mongering tweets and mindless trivia spewing from the trough of Trump's malignant vision of America and the world.

His latest vulgar, defamatory accusations and inflammatory lies; the most recent insane mass school shooting, rape or murder; Meghan Markle's baby bump: the newest dumb-ass drama in the Kardashian family; Madonna's butt implants; the first shots of Gwyneth Paltrow's stunning wedding dress.

Day in, day out, week after week, month after month, year after year, we are forced to swallow this endless stream of mind-numbing garbage shoved down our throats by the media as on the sidelines the greatest tragedy in the history of the world is taking place. The literal death of the planet. Right before our very eyes. In glorious, horrifying, living Technicolor.

If we are sensitive, if we have an ounce of feeling left within us, we shake our heads at images of a starving child dying in Yemen, its rib cage piercing its emaciated flesh, the child's weeping mother cradling the dying infant in her arms, a dead whale washed up on a beach in the Philippines, its extended stomach bloated with plastic waste, oblivious to the fact that the dirty war being waged by the Saudis in Yemen that resulted in the child's death -- a war so dirty the Saudis are recruiting young survivors of the horrors of Darfur to serve as child soldiers on the front line -- has been backed by America from the get-go, the "living hell for children" described by UNICEF that killed the starving child the consequence of diseases caused by the war; that in addition to being the world's third largest producer of oil, the U.S. is the world's third largest exporter of plastics; and that since the end of the Second World War America has ruthlessly maintained its position as the world leader in sales of another obscenely profitable, evergreen commodity.

Bombs and missiles. Weapons of war. Destruction and death.

The budget for the U.S. military signed into law by Trump in February, 2017 was $700 billion, one of the biggest increases in defense spending in American history, and the single largest expenditure on military might in the history of the world, the budget of the U.S. war machine now dwarfing that of every other nation on earth, China and Russia included, America spends more on defense than China, Russia, Saudi Arabia, the United Kingdom, India, France, Germany, Italy, Japan and Brazil combined, with over 200,000 active American troops deployed in 170 countries around the world. For decades America has dominated the global arms industry, sales figures in the fiscal year 2018 58% higher than those of its closest competitor, Russia, combined weapons sales up 13% over the previous year netting American firms $192.3 billion, their biggest clients Middle East States, Saudi Arabia topping the list.

While the American war machine continues to dominate the world's stage, leading us ever closer to the cliff of self-destruction, it has been calculated that a mere 3% of the United States military budget could wipe all starvation and poverty off the face of the earth.

America does not want to look at itself, at the nightmare it has become. And unless you are willing to wake up, neither do you. America is a nation in a permanent state of denial, a nation that has been high-jacked by a gigantic war machine, the principles and vision of the Founding Fathers so staggeringly betrayed that were George Washington, Benjamin Franklin, John Adams, Thomas Jefferson, James Madison and Thomas Paine somehow to be magically reborn, transported forward in time to the present, they would look at the state of America and the world with its endless War on Terror driven by the United States, and the shocking environmental degradation of the earth's environment in horror and weep.

Like lambs being led to the slaughter; like frogs swimming in a pot of cold water being brought to a slow, roiling boil; like proverbial lemmings sleep-walking their way toward a rapidly approaching cliff of self-destruction, relative to the timeline of earth's history, humanity is inches from complete and total annihilation.

So where does all this leave you? And where does it leave this mighty little book?

The meaning of the word 'apocalypse' has nothing to do with the end of the world. A dark Christian eschatological spin on the word projected from ignorant minds of Christian evangelicals who have similarly misunderstood and distorted the meaning of the Last Judgment and the Second Coming of Christ in the Bible, this kind of naïve, fairy tale interpretation of the visions of Daniel are as dangerous and insane as the high-jacking of Islam by ISIS.

The true meaning of the word 'apocalypse' is 'revelation'; the disclosure of secret knowledge, the revelation of that which has been hidden. Amidst all the turmoil, misery and strife, the death and disease caused by a perpetual global War on Terror, amidst the terrifying plight of the earth's environment, the way out, the truth about the true nature of the universe and human reality is being given to us now.

The Copernican Revolution began over five hundred years ago, taking more than a hundred years to complete. Nicholas Copernicus, the polymath astronomer and mathematician who started it all, was a distinguished man of the church who became so terrified by what he had discovered, the wrath he knew would rain down on his head once the Vatican learned of the heretical nature of his findings, he waited till he was on his death bed in 1543 to publish the book that would blow the Catholic church and the false, antediluvian model of the universe perpetrated by Aristotle, Plato and Ptolemy out of the water – *On the Revolutions of the Heavenly Bodies*. His book immediately placed on the Papal index of forbidden texts, it was not until almost eighty years later that the Italian polymath astronomer, physicist and engineer Galileo Galilei read a contraband copy of Copernicus' book, and finding convincing evidence in favor of the Copernican model boldly took up the fight.

Ordered by Papal injunction not "to hold, defend, or teach" the theory of Copernicus, Galileo nonetheless persisted, in 1623 publishing *Dialogue on the Two Chief Systems of the World, Ptolemaic and Copernican*, supporting the Copernican model that the earth revolves around the Sun. Threatened with torture and subjected to an eight-month trial by the Inquisition during which he was forced to "abjure, curse, and detest" the "absurd view that the earth revolved around the Sun", Galileo's book joined Copernicus' *Revolutions* on the Papal list of forbidden texts. Placed under permanent house arrest so he could be watched and prevented from causing further trouble, Galileo remained there, isolated from the world until his death in 1642.

Forty-five years later Sir Issac Newtown published his *Philosophiæ Naturalis Principia Mathematica* finally erasing any and all opposition to the revolutionary Copernican/Galilean world view, eradicating the ancient mistaken belief that the earth stood at the center of the cosmos forever.

It is my belief, and the fundamental argument of this book, that we are today in the midst of a second, far more profound and important Copernican Revolution -- a monumental breakthrough in our understanding of the human mind, the nature of reality and the universe I call **The Cosmocentric Revolution** -- because at its heart lies the revelation that the cosmos and our reality are not what they seem; that what our minds have until now perceived to be the universe is an illusion; that there is no 'out there' out there; and that we are now and have always been 100%, 24/7 the creators of our own reality, and are thus forever standing literally at the very center of the cosmos.

It is also my contention expressed in this book that the impact of what I term **The Cosmocentric Revolution** will prove to be of immeasurably greater significance than its predecessor historically, because what is at stake this time around is nothing so much bigger; nothing less than the survival of the planet and the human race. The paradigm shift is occurring not a moment too soon, as we are approaching the very brink of self-destruction, the push back from dark, controlling forces that up until now have enjoyed a virtually exclusive prerogative of the understanding and exploitation of the freedom and power contained within this profound insight into the true nature of the universe and the human mind accounting for all the darkness and confusion enveloping America, the cataclysmic mess we are in with regard to the environment, the proliferation of a culture of cruelty and violence all over the world, and the terrifying prospect of the outbreak of random nuclear war.

To the majority of people living their 'normal' day-to-day lives in the world, immersed in the prevailing materialistic worldview, statements like the ones above will seem radical, unbelievable, crazy, contradicting everything they believe that they know, running counter to common sense. To them I suggest they take some time out to review the protracted birth pangs of the Copernican Revolution and the trials and tribulations suffered by its two champions, Copernicus and Galileo.

Had you been alive during the Copernican Revolution, unless you were a radical free thinker like Copernicus and Galileo, it is unlikely you would have known it. It is the curse of scientific innovators and adventurers in creative thinking that they are always ahead of their time. As Galileo wrote, "All truths are easy to understand once they are discovered. The point is to discover them." It is the misfortune of those who discover and dare to declare any enormous paradigm shift that will change our understanding of the world before the world is ready to accept it to be harangued, mocked, persecuted and maligned.

In a letter to the Grand Duchess Christina, the daughter of Charles III of Lorraine and the grand-daughter of Catherine de Medici written because he had learned of Christina's desire to learn more about astronomy and knew that Christina's position of power would give his letter exposure to other nobles and Church leaders, Galileo described his personal experience of this truth.

"Some years ago, as Your Serene Highness well knows, I discovered in the heavens many things that had not been seen before our own age. The novelty of these things, as well as some consequences which followed from them in contradiction to the physical notions commonly held among academic philosophers, stirred up against me no small number of professors – as if I had placed these things in the sky with my own hands in order to upset nature and overturn the sciences."

"Showing a greater fondness for their own opinions than for truth, they sought to deny and disprove the new things which, if they had cared to look for themselves, their own senses would have demonstrated to them. To this end they hurled various charges and published numerous writings filled with vain arguments."

"Men who were well grounded in astronomical and physical science were persuaded as soon as they received my first message. There were others who denied them or remained in doubt only because of their novel and unexpected character, and because they had not yet had the opportunity to see for themselves. These men have by degrees come to be satisfied. But some, besides allegiance to their own error, possess I know not what fanciful interest in remaining hostile, not so much toward the things in question as toward their discoverer. No longer being able to deny them, these men now take refuge in obstinate silence, but being more than ever exasperated by that which has pacified and quieted other men, they divert their thoughts to other fancies and seek new ways to damage me."

"I should pay no more attention to them than to those who previously contradicted me – at whom I always laugh, being assured of the eventual outcome – were it not that in their new calumnies and persecutions I perceive that they do not stop at proving themselves more learned than I am, (a claim which I scarcely contest), but go so far as to cast against me the imputations of crimes which must be, and are, more abhorrent to me than death itself, persisting in their original resolve to destroy me and everything mine by any means they can think of."

"The crimes of the United States have been systematic, constant, vicious, heinous and remorseless, but very few people actually talk about them. You have to hand it to America. It has exercised a quite clinical manipulation of power worldwide while masquerading as a force for universal good. It is a brilliant, even witty, highly successful act of hypnosis. I put it to you that the United States is the greatest show on earth. Brutal, scornful, indifferent and ruthless it may be, but it is also very clever."

Harold Pinter, *Nobel Prize Acceptance Speech, 2005*

"When we hear, as we've heard throughout all our lives no matter how old we are, that we are a country that stands for freedom, for rightness, for justice for everyone, it simply doesn't apply to those who are not white. We were the most rapacious, aggressive, destructive, torturing, monstrous people who swept from one coast to the other murdering and causing mayhem among the Indians. But that isn't revealed, because we don't like that image of ourselves. We like to see ourselves as John Wayne sees us."

Marlon Brando

"The horror! The horror!"

Joseph Conrad, *Heart of Darkness*

2 AMERICAN HORROR; AMERICAN SHAME

In the chart of the United States of America drawn for the late afternoon of July 4, 1776 in Philadelphia, the date, time and place of the publication of *The Declaration of Independence,* Chiron, the asteroid symbolizing the deepest core wound of any individual or nation, the place of that individual or nation's most profound sense of inadequacy and shame, is at 20 degrees of Aries in the 4th house of America's origins, roots and ancestral heritage.

Chiron in the house of America's roots, in Aries, the sign of aggression and war, symbolizes the nation's deep-rooted shame stemming from the flood tide of violence and bloodshed, the dog-eat-dog ethics of victory at all cost, and the glorification of muscular strength that fueled the European settlers' belief in the righteousness of their drive to expand, dominate and occupy the entire North American continent out of which the nation was born. The specific degree of Aries at which Chiron is placed reflects the even harsher combative, militant rage and lust for power that the nation's hidden sense of inadequacy and shame lie buried in.

The Sabian symbols are a profound series of images representing the 360 degrees of the zodiac, channeled by a gifted clairvoyant named Elsie Wheeler almost a hundred years ago and recorded by a man who led a movement to reformulate the study of astrology in the 20th century, Marc Edmund Jones, the author of a book called *The Sabian Symbols in Astrology.*

Akin to the images inscribed in a tarot deck, or the hexagrams of the I Ching, any planet, asteroid, or angle of the chart placed at a specific degree of the zodiac magically embodies the energy of the symbol Elsie Wheeler assigned to that degree.

A harshly competitive degree of the zodiac, the Sabian symbol for America's Chiron at 20 degrees of Aries in the house of the nation's origins and roots is 'A Pugilist Enters The Ring', its keynote being the glorification of social aggressiveness, an energy that translates as the survival of the fittest aligned with a deep rooted admiration for and envy of anything or anyone capable of generating overwhelming power.

There are other energies in America's chart that reflect the nation's innate aggression, belligerence, lust for dominance and material and martial power, by far the most important being Pluto at 27 degrees of Capricorn in the nation's house of self-worth, values and money. In the following chapter, *The Sinews of War*, I go into the significance of America's Pluto placement in depth, particularly with regard to the experience of death and rebirth America finds itself grappling with today and its implications for the approaching financial collapse that will occur in 2020. For now, suffice it to say that Pluto positioned at 27 degrees of Capricorn in the 2nd house of America's chart, the sign of big business, multi-national corporations, big oil, Wall Street and the government is another symbol of America's relentless drive for expansion, material dominance and global military hegemony, as well as a crystal clear reflection of the nightmare scenario Eisenhower warned the American people of in his farewell address – the rise of the military-industrial complex and its potential domination of the nation's government led by what is today termed as the secret government, a nightmare that has since come to pass.

Pluto squares Chiron in America's chart, symbolizing the tension between this overwhelming drive for the acquisition of massive material wealth and power and the guilt and shame buried deep within America's soul at the violent, bloody nature of the crimes committed in the name of that pursuit -- primarily the appalling series of atrocities committed against Native Americans by white European immigrants in the name of 'Manifest Destiny', the widely held belief developed in the 19th century that the United States was a "chosen land" and that it was the mission and God-given right of European settlers to appropriate and colonize the entire North American continent, annihilating Native Americans, their culture and traditions in the process.

The fact that this horrific act of genocide committed against the native peoples of North America by the ancestors of men and women who govern the country today is barely mentioned in history books, let alone taught in America's public schools is a reflection of the disgrace and dishonor buried deep within the nation's soul regarding its ignominious past symbolized by Chiron in America's 4th house, the house of its origins, in the savage, brutal, warlike degree of 20 Aries.

It started with Columbus and never stopped. As the Spaniards began searching the land for gold and precious stones, looting and burning the villages of indigenous peoples that Columbus had described as "so tractable, so peaceable", and "sweet and gentle", qualities taken by the Spaniards as a sign of weakness, whole tribes were destroyed, hundreds of thousands of people murdered in less than a decade after Columbus first set foot on the beach of San Salvador on October 12, 1492, hundreds of men, women and children shipped back to Europe to be sold as slaves.

At a time when politicians and diplomats proudly proclaim that America keeps its treaties, that Americans above all are a people who keep their word, what is conveniently never taught in American schools is the dirty history of the country – that there were nearly four hundred treaties written by the United States government in good faith with the Indians, and that every single one of those treaties was abrogated, primarily as a result of European settlers' feverish lust for gold discovered on Native American lands.

"The white man made us many promises, more than I can remember", said Chief Red Cloud of the Oglala Teton Sioux, "but they never kept but one; they promised to take our land, and they took it."

The bloodcurdling massacre of the Cheyenne and the Arapaho at Sand Creek in 1864, planned and led by Colonel John M. Chivington, one of the most notorious, blood-thirsty war mongers in American history, typifies the brutal violence and needless bloodshed in the nation's past symbolized by Chiron at 20 degrees of Aries in America's 4th house.

A rapacious, brutal psychopath in charge of the Colorado regiments of the U.S. army, Chivington, a prototype of men like Dick Cheney and John Bolton, Trump's National Security Advisor, a man who spoke freely and openly of his lust for collecting the scalps of dead Indians, and of "wading knee deep in Indian gore", bulldozed his way over objections from his fellow officers that the planned assault on the peaceful Cheyenne and Arapaho camps at Sand Creek would be a violation of a pledge of safety given the Indians, murder in every sense of the word.

Becoming violently angry, Chivington reportedly slammed his fist down on a table, shouting, "Damn any man who sympathizes with Indians! I have come to kill Indians, and believe it is right and honorable to use any means under God's heaven to kill Indians!"

Two thirds of the six hundred Cheyenne and Arapaho camped at Sand Creek that day were women and children. As the American soldiers bore down on the camp most were gathered around their leader, Black Kettle, standing in front of his tepee, the American flag and the white flag of peace fluttering above it in the wind. The atrocities committed at Sand Creek that day were revolting, dishonoring the uniform of the American army – worse than those committed by the CIA and U.S. soldiers at Abu Ghraib prison in Iraq. Robert Bent, a half-Indian guide forced to ride with Chivington, gave the following eye-witness account.

"I saw five unarmed squaws hiding under a bank for shelter. When the troops came up to them they ran out, showing themselves to let the soldiers know they were women and unarmed, begging for mercy. The soldiers shot them all. I saw one squaw cut open, her unborn child lying by her side. There was an indiscriminate slaughter of men, women and children. Every dead body I saw that day was scalped, in many instances the bodies mutilated in the most horrible manner – men, women and children's private parts cut out. I saw soldiers cutting out dead women's private parts, stretching them over their saddle-bows, wearing them over their hats while riding in the ranks. I heard one soldier boast of how he had cut off the fingers of a Indian while the man was still alive to get the rings off his hand. I heard of a child a few months old being thrown into the feed-box of a wagon, being carried some distance before being tossed out and left on the ground to perish."

Pluto rules the hydrogen bomb and massive, concentrated power. In the sign of Capricorn in America's 2nd house it symbolizes the union of vast accumulated amounts of capital with mastery of the most destructive forces known to mankind. In this regard Pluto square Chiron in America's 4th house reflects how the shameful price paid for the achievement of America's vast wealth and military might by the Native Americans has continued to this day, in the century following the genocide committed against them what were once Native American lands appropriated by the government for military bases, nuclear tests, and the mining of Uranium. The current fight over the Dakota Access Pipeline waged by the Sioux at Standing Rock echoes this.

Throughout the rest of 2019, as Pluto makes its protracted return to its exact position in America's chart for the first time in the nation's history the planet's implacable, take-no-prisoners energy is battering America's Chiron, ripping away the flimsy band aid covering the nation's hidden sense of shame, forcing America to face its deepest, darkest secrets, its most profound core issues, all of which in some way have their roots in and are connected to the horrific crimes committed against the Native Americans that culminated two centuries ago in the name of the white European man's 'Manifest Destiny'.

One hardly need be a rocket scientist to hear the transparent echoes of the white-supremacist concept of 'Manifest Destiny' in the ultra-aggressive strategic foreign policy of John Bolton, a policy virtually identical to that laid out in the founding statement and principles of *The Project For the New American Century*, the neoconservative think tank founded by Dick Cheney, Donald Rumsfeld, Paul Wolfowitz and George W. Bush that drove America's invasion of Iraq and Afghanistan after 9/11 – or to hear the same echoes in the title of Cheney's autobiography, *Exceptional: Why the World Needs a Powerful America,* and the cheesy parody of Reagan's drum beat Trump literally hung his hat on as he lied and bullied his way to victory in the election, *Make America Great Again.*

The biggest winners from the War on Terror, unsurprisingly, have been America's largest defense contractors and oil servicing companies, in the years since the War on Terror was declared annual salaries for the CEOs of America's biggest defense contractors trebling to a combined total of over $1.5 billion, enough to cover the wages of three million Iraqis for a year. The wars in Iraq and Afghanistan have been a massive financial boon for the U.S. arms industry, contracts held by Cheney's alma mater as CEO, Halliburton, jumping more than nine times, from $400 million to $3.9 billion, Northrop Grumman's doubling, and the largest American arms company, Lockheed Martin seeing an increase of over 50%, from $14.7 billion to $21.9 billion.

It is estimated that by the end of 2019 the total cost of the War on Terror will stand at approximately $6.5 trillion, an obscene number – but that cost cannot be calculated simply from columns on a ledger. From the American soldiers and Iraqi civilians killed, maimed, or displaced by the violence, to the children who play on roads and in fields sown with improvised explosive devices and cluster bombs, no numbers will ever come close to conveying the devastating toll in human lives and psychological damage of the wars in Iraq and Afghanistan, nor the cost of those wars spilling over into the neighboring states of Syria and Pakistan, nor the cost of those wars coming home to the United States in the form of the disabled and wounded.

Due to the high rates of injuries over half of the 2.5 million men and women who served in Iraq and Afghanistan have returned to the U.S. suffering some degree of disability, the cost of their health care and benefits estimated to amount to more than $1 trillion over the coming decades.

Classified U.S. military documents released by Wikileaks in October, 2010 revealed a total death toll to that date of over 109,000 in Iraq, more than 66,000 of them Iraqi civilians. As of 2019 over 15,000 American soldiers and contractors have been killed, over 32,000 troops wounded in action, roughly 380,000 Iraqi, Afghanistan, and Pakistan civilians dead.

In the same vein, while *The Wall Street Journal* reported in October 2018 that faster, increased military spending by the government was responsible for almost 50% of the acceleration in America's economic growth since mid-2017, the party won't last. Over time military spending is known to negatively impact every nation's economic growth, and to be particularly detrimental to the economies of wealthier countries, over a 20-year period, a 1% increase in military spending decreasing a wealthy nation's economic growth by as much as 9%. Not surprisingly, given all of the above, the big take away from the symbolism of Pluto in Capricorn in America's 2nd house of money and wealth square Chiron at 20 degrees of Aries in the 4th, and the fast approaching return of Pluto to its natal position in America's chart for the first time in history – a take away which I get into in greater detail in the following chapter -- is that America is a country on the verge of self-destruction, bankrupting itself, primarily from decades of accumulated, bloated military spending.

The return of Pluto to its natal place triggering the natal square to Chiron in America's chart is screaming, "Change your life, America! Change your ways! Face your darkness! Face your shame! Transcend, transmute, get honest, or perish!"

What is America? What is the nation's truth? How far has it strayed from its deepest values? What is the country's capacity for honestly, openly confronting and transmuting the profound sense of shame buried deep within the nation's soul so that America can be reborn? All of these questions are bubbling up to the surface in the collective American psyche at this time, demanding to be answered. America is riddled with intense, deep-rooted guilt. And not just over the appalling atrocities committed against the Native Americans. This wound is profound, extending back to the ignominy of the country's history of slavery, and to every single political travesty and horror committed over the course of the past century that has never been brought to light, the dark, dirty history of duplicity and skullduggery that lies buried deep within the collective American soul.

In this regard it is my belief it will not only be the shocking truth behind the multiple criminal travesties of Trump and his family that will be brought to the light between now and 2023 as America experiences its protracted death and rebirth -- but the heinous truth about 9/11, the assassinations of JFK, his brother Bobby, Dr. Martin Luther King, and the whole history of political and financial chicanery that has gone on in America over the past one hundred years -- since the creation of the Federal Reserve in 1913 – a history that is only now reaching its tragic, sordid climax, the systematic rape, abuse and pillage of the American people by special interest groups dominated by the banking industry, the CIA and the military-industrial complex, and big oil, supported by their champions in Washington, the most corrupt incarnation of the Republican party in the nation's history.

"There is no coming to consciousness without pain", wrote the great doctor of the soul, Carl Gustav Jung. In mythology, Chiron is the wounded healer, representative of the seed of spiritual transformation and the potential for the achievement of wisdom through suffering. The energy of alchemical transcendence, its astrological symbol is a key, signifying that by summoning the courage to unlock the power of Chiron through open, honest self-reflection and spiritual enquiry, the transmutation of deep inner suffering and shame, a portal will open up to profound wisdom, power and inner peace.

Chiron is the master of wisdom through suffering. Correctly navigated, Pluto's transit to Chiron in America's chart will be the force that heralds the dawning of Lady Liberty's bright and brilliant, brand new day.

"One of the generals who used to work for me called me in. He says, 'We've made the decision we're going to war with Iraq.' I said, 'We're going to war with Iraq? Why?' He said, I don't know. I guess they don't know what else to do. This is a memo that describes how we're going to take out seven countries in five years, starting with Iraq, and then Syria, Lebanon, Libya, Somalia, Sudan and, finishing off, Iran. I guess if the only tool you have is a hammer, every problem has to look like a nail.'"

General Wesley Clark recounting a conversation in the Pentagon with one of the generals of the Joint Chiefs of Staff four weeks after 9/11

"The new American realism, which is nothing other than gross corporate power cloaked in demagogy, means one thing only: that America will put America first in everything,"

John Le Carré, *The Tailor of Panama*

"Nothing will avail to offset this virus which is poisoning the whole world. America is the very incarnation of doom. She will drag the whole world down to the bottomless pit."

Henry Miller, *Tropic of Cancer*

"Endless money forms the sinews of war."

Marcus Tullius Cicero

3 THE SINEWS OF WAR

In the great seal of the United States on the back of a dollar bill the eagle clutches an olive branch with thirteen leaves in its right claw, thirteen arrows clutched in its left, the eagle's head turned away from the arrows, towards the symbol of peace.

Thirteen stands for the number of original American states. The eagle's head facing the olive branch, away from the arrows, is deeply symbolic. The Founding Fathers were determined America would stand as a bold, proud, fierce new nation founded on the principles of liberty, freedom, justice, and, in the words of the principal designer of the great seal, Charles Thomson, "the power of peace". The eagle was armed and ready to defend itself, but the nation's attention was to be directed towards the virtues and spirit of peace.

The Founding Fathers were men of deep spiritual faith and intellect, as well as bona fide statesmen. Staunch defenders of the practice and propagation of civic virtue, dedicated to the high politics and integrity of statesmanship and the absolute need of the human spirit for freedom, they were sons of the Enlightenment, humanists and free thinkers – a billion miles from the self-absorbed, self-aggrandizing American political elite of today. Every one of them saw themselves as the grand architects and engineers of a nation that would lead the world in a new order of the ages embodying the values, ideals, ethics, morality and character that define the idealized vision of America the American people are struggling to believe still exists today.

Since the end of the Second World War and the creation of the CIA, the institution that became the heart of America's secret government, the nightmare scenario Eisenhower warned of in his farewell address citing the potential for the "disastrous rise of misplaced power", what he termed the military-industrial complex ballooning into a rapacious monster of staggering proportions, has come to pass, 9/11 and the events that followed leading to the eagle's head on the great seal being permanently turned in the opposite direction, away from the olive branch to face the arrows, America dragging the rest of the world into a state of perpetual global war.

James Madison, the fourth President of the United States, a man who played a pivotal role in the drafting of the *American Constitution* and the *Bill of Rights*, wrote the following words about the perils to America presented by the prospect of war.

"Of all the enemies to public liberty war is to be the most dreaded, because it comprises and develops the germ of every other. War is the parent of armies; from these proceed debts and taxes, and armies, debts, and taxes are the known instruments for bringing the many under the domination of the few. In war, the discretionary power of the Executive is extended, its influence in dealing out offices, honors and emoluments multiplied -- and all the means of seducing the minds are added to those of subduing the force of the people. The same malignant aspect in republicanism may be traced in the inequality of fortunes, and the opportunities of fraud growing out of a state of war, and in the degeneracy of manners and morals engendered by both. No nation could preserve its freedom in the midst of continual warfare."

In his recent books *American Nightmare*, *America at War with Itself*, and *The Violence of Organized Forgetting*, the brilliant American/Canadian scholar and cultural critic Henry A. Giroux makes the repeated point that the social and economic issues threatening to strangle the original concept of democracy in America as conceived by the Founding Fathers are no accident, but the result of a deliberate, organized attempt to high-jack the integrity of their vision in the post 9/11 world.

The increase in the dehumanization and militarization of society, the glorification of war and the military pervading every aspect of popular culture, aggressive militarism, war-like values and hyper-masculinity dominating everything from movies, music and video games, to intermissions at major league football games; the creeping, insidious acceptance of violence, cruelty, pornography and ignorance as acceptable social norms; the assault on higher education, schools and universities increasingly defunded, devalued and privatized, turned into accountability factories designed to mimic the values and the culture of casino capitalism; the general hardening of the culture and the emergence of a social order driven by the collapse of ethics and an unchecked celebration of self-interest are disturbing symptoms of the rise of a neoliberal form of organized gangster capitalism more aptly termed neoliberal fascism, the hallmarks of which are violence, cruelty, the celebration of a dog-eat-dog mentality, and greed.

Under the fifty year-long plus reign of neoliberal fascism in America the principles of freedom, self-expression, and compassion that were the core of the Founding Fathers' vision have been mocked, trivialized and sidelined, self-interest, greed and the mentality of the survival of the fittest enthroned as a national ideal.

As I pointed out in the last chapter, the United States has a long history with the culture of cruelty, violence and greed that has repeatedly undermined and challenged its hollow claims to be the embodiment of liberty, equality, freedom, compassion and justice that define a true democracy, a history by no means uniquely symbolized by the policies and behavior of the Trump administration.

Prior to Trump's election the culture of cruelty, violence and greed resided on the margins of power, concealed beneath the empty, shallow rhetoric of conservative and liberal politicians who, while mouthing their pretentions to the principles of democracy, were covertly exploiting the well-oiled machinery of government, big business and Wall Street to advance their own interests, power and private agendas while feathering the nests of their colleagues, supporters and friends amongst the ultra-rich elite.

With Trump holding the reins of power the gloves are off, his full-frontal, unabashed embrace of the culture of selfishness, cruelty, violence and greed blatantly driving policies ramping up the hitherto covert process of the dehumanization and militarization of America —a dark energy that views basic human emotions such as compassion, empathy and care for others, and the fragility and beauty of the earth's environment with disdain. How else can one explain the $1.5 trillion tax cut benefitting primarily the ultra-rich and corporations and the obscene increase in military spending in Trump's budget, together with his determination to sabotage every attempt by the global community to tackle the ever increasing threat of an environmental apocalypse driven by global warming that now more than ever is showing itself imminent on the horizon? The culture of violence and war now colors every facet of American life, including schools, the Trump administration's school safety report released in December, 2018, encouraging school districts to consider arming teachers with guns, praising state programs that arm teachers and suggesting schools could access federal funds to train staff in the use of firearms.

In his best-selling book on global economics, *Capital in the Twenty-first Century*, the French economist Thomas Pikkety noted 60% of the increase in American national income between 1977 and 2007 went exclusively to the top 1% earners, the only section of the population surpassing them the top 10th of that 1%, the top 100th of that top 1% doing the best of all. Piketty believes this trend towards greater inequality in wealth will continue, returns from capital growing faster than the economy, faster than the owners of that wealth will be able to spend it.

Pikkety's book was published in 2013. One only has to look at Trump's tax bill to see how right he was. Described as "the biggest wealth grab in modern history" by *Fortune Magazine*, it is estimated that the richest 5% of Americans will receive 61% of Trump's tax cuts, the bottom 60% a meagre 14%. Many of those men and women in the category of the 5% richest and the majority of those ranked in the top 1% have dramatically increased their fortunes over the past seventeen years, directly or indirectly, as a result of the War on Terror – and it has not been merely via the "opportunities for fraud growing out of a state of war" stated by James Madison that they have managed to do so. Through shrewd exploitation of their investments in the armaments and oil service industries and the vast network of countless new ancillary private businesses providing security, intelligence and logistical services in support of the war and its effects on American society literally billions upon billions have been made, America's War on Terror playing a dominant role in accelerating the already enormous gap between the super-rich and those less fortunate, for the wealthiest Americans the War on Terror being nothing less than the equivalent of hitting the jackpot in Vegas.

At the conclusion of the last chapter I made the point that the symbolic take away from Pluto in Capricorn in America's house of money and wealth squaring Chiron at 20 degrees of Aries in the 4th, and the fast approaching return of Pluto, lord of destruction and rebirth to its natal position for the first time in history is that the country is on the verge of bankrupting itself as a result of decades of binge spending on military expansion and the quest for global dominance. The other factor feeding into the oncoming inevitable financial collapse is symbolized in America's chart by Pluto opposite Mercury in the 8th the house of shared resources – the climax of a two hundred and fifty year obsession with the accumulation of limitless financial power -- in a single word, greed. In this chapter I am going to delineate the trajectory of America's death and rebirth, which will be primarily financially driven. Again, my point is not to scare you, but to get you to open up your eyes, take back the power and prepare for what will inevitably come to pass so that you are ready. First, however, it is important to understand some of the more esoteric facets of America's chart

In astrology fixed stars -- the stars we see in the sky at night termed 'fixed' because although they progress over time, they are so far away relative to the earth they appear to hardly move – are known to have a great deal of influence on the nature and character of any person or nation if they are emphasized in that person or nation's chart. Since the end of the Second World War two of the most warlike, bellicose energies in the entire pantheon of fixed stars have progressed to a point where they are now fused with the ruling planets of war in America's chart – Pluto and Mars.

Fused with Pluto is the fixed star Terebellum, a star which in terms of America's nuclear ambitions and the agenda of the military-industrial complex has turned the United States into a volatile, explosive country ready to take over and dominate any situation in the world whenever and wherever the opportunity presents itself, using cunning, guile and deceit to exploit any opening that will enable America to control the world – an America brazenly comfortable with forcefully pulling down any nation or organization that attempts to challenge its ambitions.

The violent, mercenary energy of Terebellum has been reinforced by the fixed star now fused with America's Mars – Bellatrix. Another energy of hostility, Bellatrix is a star associated with a love of leading others into fights and the sadistic pleasure derived from acts of cruelty (think of the horrendous images of the CIA officials and American soldiers heartlessly torturing Iraqi prisoners inside Abu Ghraib prison.) Bellatrix on Mars in America's chart has created a nation permanently hungering for the development of one violent situation after another to satisfy its bottomless, twisted bloodlust. It is no accident that the energies of Terebellum on America's Pluto and Bellatrix on the nation's Mars have intensified since the most heinous crime in American history was committed on September 11, the United States leading the world down a path of endless war with the launch of the War of Terror.

Talk of the next big financial meltdown has been rife for years, the boom/bust cycles of the global economy an accepted fact of life. It is thought that when the next collapse of the U.S. economy occurs it will happen quickly and that no one can predict its timing, because the signs of imminent failure are hard to see. The signs in America's chart are crystal clear, however, and delineated for you below.

September 15, 2018 was the 10th anniversary of the collapse of Lehman Brothers, the fourth-largest investment bank in the United States, a defining moment that pushed the U.S. economy into the worst crisis since the 1930s. The current direction in federal policy suggests it is priming to happen again, and that is reflected in America's chart.

With the deregulation of the financial sector, ten banks too big to fail, J.P. Morgan, Goldman Sachs and Citigroup among them, owning more than 50% of the assets of the top 100 commercial banks, Trump's attacks on the Federal Reserve leading to uncertainty over the Feds future policy, the knock-on effect of which could potentially be the return of stagflation not seen since the Nixon years, and the revolving door between Wall Street and Washington spinning faster than ever, the risks of a financial collapse bigger than 2008 have never been higher. And given the truth of the maxim 'the bigger they are, the harder they fall', if deregulation should lead to a worst-case scenario, that list of ten banks mentioned above will fall even harder this time around.

When the perfect financial storm occurs, the policy tools for addressing it this time around won't be there. Overwhelming public debt, any innovative financial remedies hamstrung by inflated balance sheets and lack of room to cut policy rates, with the top ten too big to fail banks owning more than 50% of the assets of the top 100 commercial banks, unlike in 2008, the government will have its hands tied as overall debt levels soar way higher than those during the previous crisis.

As Pluto returns to its exact natal position in America's chart at the beginning 2020 it is joined by Saturn, the planet of blowback and karma in direct opposition with Mercury in the 8th house of shared resources (Wall Street/the Federal Reserve). Even under the best of circumstances this combination of energies, which repeats in October/November, represents the onset of an intense, protracted financial depression. Because Mercury in the chart is conjunct the fixed star Procyon, a star that brings wealth brought about by will-power and the ability to put bold ideas into action followed by a disastrous self-inflicted fall, these periods of time will be harder to navigate. In addition to this, Saturn's conjunction with natal Pluto in America's chart occurring at roughly the same time, an energy that last hit America during the depression of 1991, supported by Pluto's opposition to Mercury symbolizes the collapse of the existing financial order, social upheaval, political instability and unrest, severe limitations placed on the nation's financial resources.

What will begin as a crack in one wall of a single building will cascade into first the building, then the entire block's wholesale collapse.

In the preceding chapter I described the Sabian symbol for America's Chiron at 20 degrees of Aries. The Sabian symbol for the point in America's chart called the Vertex, the point known as the degree of fate, at 26 degrees of Cancer, next to Mercury in the house of shared resources which Saturn opposes on America's financial axis in the early months of 2020 and again in the late fall, an opposition Pluto repeats in 2021 – delivers a stunning confirmation of what in 2020 will occur.

The Sabian symbol for America's Vertex is 'A Violent Storm in a Canyon', the keynote being a confrontation with a social upheaval demanding the reconsideration of static, outdated values. In 2020 the ruling elite of America will be forced to see their position and security destroyed by forces beyond their control, undergoing a profound metamorphosis as the result of a crisis produced by uncontrollable karmic forces.

"However political parties may now and then answer popular ends they are likely in the course of time to become potent engines by which cunning, ambitious, and unprincipled men will be enabled to subvert the power of the people and to usurp for themselves the reins of government, destroying afterwards the very engines which have lifted them to unjust dominion."

George Washington's Farewell Address

"A nation can survive its fools and the ambitious. But it cannot survive treason from within. For the traitor appears not a traitor. He speaks in the accents familiar to his victims, and he appeals to the baseness that lies deep in the hearts of men. He rots the soul of a nation. He infects the body politic so it can no longer resist. A murderer is less to be feared.

Marcus Tullius Cicero

"The tyrant is a child of pride, who drinks from his sickening cup of recklessness and vanity, until from his high crest headlong he plummets to the dust of hope."

Sophocles, *Oedipus Rex*

"Donald pisses ice water."

Roy Cohn, Trump's deceased legal counsel

4 HEART OF DARKNESS

We live in a world where the divisions between the rich and the poor have never been greater. While men of vast wealth, like Bill Gates, possess more money than literally all of Africa, two thirds of the world's children live in poverty. What this level of extreme financial inequality has been proven to create is a shallow, self-perpetuating culture of superiority, narcissism and entitlement, the primary hallmark of which is a significant increase in exploitative, illegal behavior – unethical people stealing and benefiting from things they are not entitled to on behalf of those possessing the most wealth in order to maintain and increase their disproportionate power.

Termed the "asshole effect" by psychologist Paul K. Piff, this insatiable lust for excess spawned by the experience of power is the very definition of avarice, the opposite of 'noblesse oblige', the time-honored, unwritten obligation of privileged men and women to act kindly, honorably and generously towards those less fortunate than themselves. Tragically pervasive in today's society, nowhere can it be seen more clearly than in the character, life and Presidency of Donald J. Trump.

In the summer of 2018 I was introduced to a man who at one time worked closely with Trump and his children. I mentioned the book I was writing, my analysis of Trump's character according to the information in his chart, and the inevitable, rapidly approaching, stunning end to his career we are about to witness detonate in 2019, 2020 and beyond.

The man listened carefully, quietly confirming each of my observations about Trump's narcissistic, cold-hearted, venal soul as I made them, amazed that I could pinpoint the character of a man I had never met simply by studying the planets, asteroids and fixed stars in his astrological chart.

I concluded my summary of Trump's psychological profile with a single incisive sentence. "Trump has the chart of a mendacious, malignant psychopath."

"You've nailed him to a tee," the man told me. "Trump's a sick, twisted asshole. A narcissistic, heartless bastard." Then, echoing the words of Trump's infamous deceased ex-attorney, Roy Cohn, Trump's mentor in the art of shamelessness and duplicity, a master of character assassination, a lawyer completely lacking any kind of moral compass, a man whom Trump admiringly called "vicious" and "brutal", a "guy who brutalizes for you", the man concluded, "Donald pisses ice water."

In this chapter I am going to provide an in-depth study of the character and psychology of Trump according to his chart, not only because Trump's fate is indelibly bound up with the death and rebirth of America, but to prove my point that, as Jung noted, without committing to a path of spiritual growth via deep, honest self-examination and self-appraisal, intentionally coming to consciousness by bringing their inner darkness to the light, an individual has no free will, the energies in their chart playing out precisely as they are written, as if it was their fate, as if they were the stars' tennis-balls.

Like attracts like. To understand Trump, it helps to first understand Roy Cohn, his mentor. Senator Joseph McCarthy's chief counsel and hatchet man during the communist witch hunt of the 1950s, Roy Cohn made a huge impression on Trump, from the early '70s until his death in the mid '80s serving as Teflon Blondie's lethal legal counsel. Infamous for his remorseless tactics of threats, counterattacks and intimidation, Cohn reinforced in Trump the value of his innate ability to induce fear in his opponents by sheer, vicious, brass-knuckled bullying.

"When you attack Donald, he punches back ten times harder", Melania Trump remarked during the 2016 election campaign.

A fervent admirer of Cohn's pitiless, slash-and-burn legal style, in his ferocious pit-bull lawyer Trump found a mentor in another area of business he was already naturally skilled at, duplicity and fraud, the admit nothing, deny everything code of conduct we have witnessed Trump religiously adhere to every time he has been accused of any moral, ethical or legal transgression either prior to, or during his tenure of office.

Acquitted three times in federal court during the '70s and '80s on criminal charges ranging from bribery, to witness tampering, perjury, conspiracy and fraud, in 1986 a five judge panel of the New York Supreme

Court disbarred Cohn for life for unethical and unprofessional conduct, including lying on a bar application, the misappropriation of funds, and for pressuring a client to amend his will, forcing a pen into the dying man's hand in his hospital room in an attempt to make himself his client's primary beneficiary.

Following his fall, Trump hosted a lavish dinner party for Cohn in Manhattan, subsequently giving his loyal, butcherly lawyer a taste of his own medicine, distancing himself from his vicious mentor before dropping him altogether when he discovered Cohn had contracted HIV and was dying of AIDS.

"I can't believe he's doing this to me", Cohn was quoted as saying on his death bed. "Donald pisses ice water."

In recent years a great deal of research has been done on the neurobiology of sociopaths, individuals incapable of feeling any empathy -- in the majority of cases of feeling any kind of emotion at all beyond anger and rage -- people completely lacking remorse for their criminal actions, comfortable with exploiting others for their personal gain while experiencing a grandiose, deluded belief in their intellectual, moral and physical superiority.

There is a fine line between the definition of a sociopath and a psychopath, the primary distinction being that sociopaths typically exhibit a less extreme lack of empathy and guilt than psychopaths, under certain conditions being capable of forming deep bonds, with their families for example, allowing them to feel guilt or remorse if they hurt someone they love, something the classic psychopath finds it impossible to do.

The other major distinction is that the classic psychopath is much more highly organized in his criminal thinking, and can con and manipulate others with his charisma and intimidation tactics with ease, mimicking emotions he doesn't feel, but that are considered "normal" to society highly effectively. Keenly aware that what they are doing is wrong, psychopaths don't care. It is estimated approximately 93% of psychopaths wind up in the criminal justice system.

It is my contention, supported by the data in his chart, that Trump straddles the fine line between the sociopath and the psychopath, but that as the events of 2019, 2020 and thereafter inevitably unfold, he will go down in history permanently and irrefutably remembered as a classic psychopath.

One of the strongest symptoms of our collective psychosis is that as a society we have become fascinated by psychopaths, twisted characters like Frank Underwood, Patrick Bateman, and Dexter Morgan dominating our TV and movie screens. "A people that elects corrupt politicians, imposters, thieves and traitors are not victims, but accomplices", wrote George Orwell. The character of a nation's President reflects the morality and preoccupations of the nation's culture and times. It is no accident Trump began his climb to political power in the era of *American Psycho* and *Dexter*, winning the election as *House of Cards* was at the height of its popularity.

It is also no coincidence that Kevin Spacey, the star of *House of Cards*, an actor I knew and worked with on stage in New York thirty-seven years ago, has suffered a stunning fall from grace, decades of his anti-social, sexually abusive behavior exposed and brought to light, becoming a social pariah at the very moment one of the most corrupt, immoral Presidents in American history is on the point of suffering an identical fate.

With capitalism structured to richly reward precisely the kind of ruthless, cut-throat behavior typified by psychopaths now more than ever, it is hardly surprising that recent studies have found one in five corporate professionals display significant psychopathic traits, clinical psychopaths estimated to make up as many as 4% of American corporate CEOs, many of whom stand a high probability of spending significant time behind bars in the course of their lifetimes. While psychopaths account for a relatively small percentage of America's general population, their prevalence in committing crimes means they account for an estimated 15-25% of the male prison population.

Below is a checklist of the traits of a classic psychopath.

Callousness. A total lack of empathy for the feelings of others.

A high tolerance for revulsion and disgust.

Shallow emotions.

Zero capacity for shame, embarrassment, guilt, or remorse.

Sexual promiscuity.

Irresponsibility.

Recklessness.

Blame externalization. Blaming others for their own mistakes.

Only ever admitting blame when forced into a corner.

Pathological lying.

Glibness. Superficial charm.

Boastfulness. Grandiosity.

Pathological egocentricity.

Selfishness. A total incapacity for love.

Volatility. Unpredictability. Inability to plan for the future.

Violence. A low threshold for discharge of aggression.

A constant need for stimulation and admiration.

Criminal versatility. Cunning.

Possessing an extremely adept ability for manipulation.

Poor behavioral controls.

Ladies and gentlemen, I give you the President of the United States of America.

No matter what you feel about Trump – no matter how horrified, vilified and revolted you are by his personality and his policies and the reprehensible behavior of his Republican criminal cronies, it is an undeniable fact that he is a perfect reflection of the virus ailing America, the collective identity crisis and spiritual psychosis that has the nation by its throat, and in this regard is the ideal President for his time. This is how and why Trump's demise is directly related to the death and rebirth of America.

As I wrote in my introduction, at long last the emperor in America has no clothes. In Trump's bullying arrogance, his despicable, sordid clamor to turn the office of the Chief Executive of the United States into a cheap, vulgar reality show, a blatantly self-serving dictatorship, he is unconsciously abetting what for decades has been the inevitable oncoming collapse of a corrupt, decaying, dying system.

Trump is nothing. He's a symptom, not the cause. A bloated, grotesque, shameful symbol of America's profound spiritual and moral malaise, he will shortly be consigned to the scrap heap of history, his only legacy that of being remembered as one of the most ignominious Presidents since the nation's birth. Trump's presence in the Oval office is only of any significance because he stands as the perfect mirror of the sickness reflected in the nation's chart erupting like a slowly bursting bubble of pathological poison that has lain buried deep within the American soul for a very long time.

Reading an astrological chart at the level I practice is like having a person standing psychologically naked before me. As Jung understood it, the chart is a map of someone's soul; a mythological drawing of the complexity of that person's psyche. When I study an astrological chart I see everything about the person before me.

Everything.

The epitome of a demagogue, a con artist par excellence possessing a genius for manipulation and fraud, deceiving many of his business partners in the same way he has seduced, beguiled and intimidated the American people and his feeble, corrupt, gutless cronies in the Republican party, the same way he used the phony excuse of bone spurs to cowardly dodge the draft in the '60s, Trump's chart describes a man with massive character flaws rooted in extensive karmic debt he has racked up over the course of many lifetimes. Despite the surface appearances — the money, the business empire, the women, the power – Trump is a man who has maxed out every credit card in his spiritual wallet; a man who has shot his spiritual wad; a man whose fast approaching, unavoidable end will not be pretty.

Deeply unconscious, unconcerned with the depth of the depravity and darkness deep within his soul, in Jungian terms his shadow, his big black bag, which because of his ego and lazy, venal nature he has allowed to dominate his life, whenever a person like Trump spends an entire lifetime avoiding a confrontation with their dark side, they wind up projecting it onto others.

"Loser!" "Idiot!" "Rapists!" Bad hombres!" "Fake news! Phony stuff!" "He's got a pathological temper!" "Comey's a show-boater! A grandstander!" "Germany is a captive of Russia!" "Why are we having all these people from shithole countries come here?!"

All the above, a random selection of the countless ugly, nasty aspersions he has cast on other people and nations during the course of his three years in office are classic examples of Trump's shadow projection – his projection onto others of what he secretly believes about himself, which he prefers to keep hidden inside his big black bag, refusing to bring them to the light and own them. Because of this, when his nefarious deeds and the heinous hidden elements of his personality are brought forcibly to the light by Pluto in 2019, 2020 and beyond, what will occur in Trump's life and in the life of the United States of America will be the equivalent of a 9.5 earthquake on the Richter scale, the aftershocks rippling around the world.

Trump was born with his Gemini Sun (Twitter/the media/television) conjunct (fused with) Uranus (genius/anarchy), and the North Node of the Moon (popularity) in the house of his career and public destiny, supported by Jupiter (faith/abundance) in the house of his self-worth and money, and a punchy, braggadocio Mars (aggression/war) in the flashy, showy sign of Leo conjunct his ascendant (Trump's personality/image/physical body).

Anyone with this kind of set up arrives on the planet with a built-in, shock-proof faith in their own genius, a keen awareness they have a unique, exciting destiny ahead of them, a taste for dangerous, flamboyant risk-taking combining with a strength of belief and will-to-power that, come what come may, they will manifest their dreams. Trump believed in himself 100% from the get-go, convinced of his own superiority, knowing without question no matter what he wanted to achieve, no matter how many times he crossed the line and put himself above the law, whatever he put his mind to, he would succeed at it on a grand scale. That is fundamentally how and why he is now the 45th President of the United States.

Trump's relentless faith in himself and what he arrogantly, erroneously believes to be his innate superiority, combined with his remorseless, furious desire for revenge at all cost in the teeth of every betrayal and humiliation public or private he has ever experienced, (watch the video of Trump's face as he listens to the scathing speeches mocking his ambitions to become the President delivered by Seth Myers and Barack Obama at the 2011 White House Correspondents Dinner), fueled his absolute refusal to see any obstacles in his path to victory in the election with a rabid intensity, and hence he won it. Richard Branson has recounted how in the '90s, out of curiosity, thinking they would have "an interesting conversation about a whole range of issues", he accepted an invitation to lunch with Trump, only to discover all Trump was interested in talking about was how his life's mission from then on was going to be to destroy the lives of five people he had called on for help who had refused to lend him money when one his companies filed for bankruptcy.

Many of my countless anti-Trump readers will no doubt take exception to me affirming there is an aspect of genius to Trump. It is nonetheless a fact, and like everything else about the man, to any astrologer of any ability and intelligence a fact that is crystal clear from his chart. A coarse, arrogant, egomaniacal psychopath he may be, but he is also a brilliant, street-wise con-man and demagogue who instinctively knows how to brand and sell himself to the masses, getting exactly what he wants from his supporters with the minimum of effort, like another famous demagogue who could manipulate a crowd like no other man of his time.

Adolf Hitler.

Jupiter is the energy of abundance, expansion and excess, as well as at a deeper level faith. Whichever house the planet falls in is the area where a person or nation will experience an easy flow of abundance and good fortune -- no matter how ugly, or dark the energy of their horoscope is elsewhere. Having Jupiter in his house of money and self-worth in support of his triple Sun/Uranus/North Node conjunction in the house of his career means that for Trump making money from a splashy, successful business was always going to be an easy ride.

What lies beneath, however, is something very different.

Like America, Trump was born with Chiron, the asteroid symbolizing his deepest sense of self-doubt, vulnerability, inadequacy and shame, in a very challenging position. In the case of Trump, Chiron sits less than three degrees away from that exuberant, abundant Jupiter in the same house of his personal income and self-esteem conjunct a fixed star called Algorab, The Crow, a star associated with lying, scavenging, destructiveness, malevolence, fiendishness and repulsiveness, translating in Trump's case as a deep-rooted, obsessive fear he has kept hidden from the world his entire life.

Deep down inside Trump is a duplicitous, malignant scavenger, secretly fearing he is worth nothing.

All the gaudiness, the vulgarity, the brash, obsessive show with money, being the biggest, the greatest and the best stems from this unconscious dread he has kept buried deep down inside all his life that he is fundamentally, just like those African countries, a "shithole". Deep in his heart of hearts, Trump believes he is a "loser" – which is why we so frequently hear him projecting that ugly, secret, dark thought onto others, spitting out that childish, abusive curse at everyone he hates, or who has ever dared to cross him.

And it is from that same unconscious self-belief his history of rampant sexual abuse of women stems.

44

Trump's chart, like the charts of Harvey Weinstein and Kevin Spacey, depicts a classic, deeply insecure, covert sexual predator and narcissist with serious daddy/mommy issues — and with Mars, the god of war in the sign of Leo (the showman) on his Ascendant (again his body/image), he is an obnoxious, pugnacious, angry street fighter with a cruel, vicious tongue, and a hair-trigger temper.

In a nutshell Trump's chart is that of a perverse, classic playground bully who loves nothing better than to get his rocks off by verbally and physically abusing others, forever spoiling for a fight. Indeed, in his chart he lives for these things. He relishes speaking his mind, doesn't give a damn what anyone thinks, gets bored out of his mind in a heartbeat, and loves nothing better than the adrenaline rush and thrill of provoking another fight, taking another risk. And as with any man or woman with a wildly overinflated, out of control ego, Trump's greatest strengths will ultimately bring him to his knees. Hence Putin and Russia. Hence Stormy Daniels. Hence the Playboy model. Hence the Trump World Tower employee with whom he has been rumored to have fathered an illegitimate child. Hence the nineteen women who have come forward accusing him of sexual harassment and assault. And hence the "Jane Doe" who in 2016 filed a $100 million lawsuit against Trump in which she claimed he had repeatedly raped her over a four-month period when she was barely thirteen at a series of underage sex parties hosted by Trump's friend, the convicted billionaire pedophile, Jeffrey Epstein.

The "Jane Doe", who claimed Trump made her dress up in a blonde wig so that she would resemble his daughter Ivanka, later dropped her lawsuit when, like Stormy Daniels, she received death threats against herself and her family. Like Stormy Daniels, Trump's "Jane Doe" nightmare is not going to go away. Every one of the scurrilous rumors are true, including the most salacious part of the Steele dossier recounting how Trump hired a group of Russian hookers so he could watch them peeing on each other in the bed in which Barack and Michelle Obama had slept at the Ritz-Carlton in Moscow.

This chapter on the energies in Trump's chart that depict the deep pathological darkness in his soul is called *Heart of Darkness* for a reason. The central idea of the novella of the same name by Joseph Conrad, one of the greatest writers in the English language and the inspiration for Francis Ford Coppola's award-winning film, *Apocalypse Now*, is that to this day there is fundamentally no difference between many civilized people and savages.

A study of the fixed stars in Trump's chart confirms this. Below I list the other fixed stars in Trump's chart apart from Algorab on his Chiron that so perfectly define the flaws in his character which, because he has chosen to

45

avoid his spiritual journey in this lifetime, will in 2019, 2020 and beyond bring him to his knees

Alfard

Positioned on Trump's Mars (aggression/war) and his Ascendant (his persona/physical body/the way he projects his energy), Alfard gives Trump his strong passions, lack of self-control, great troubles, anxiety and loss in connection with real estate and buildings (Trump's multiple corporate bankruptcies), immorality, addictions to and revolting deeds involving women, and poisonous hatred received from those women as a result.

Alnilam

Positioned on Trump's Sun (the core of his being), Alnilam makes for a rash, headstrong, treacherous nature, bringing him notoriety and fleeting fame.

Bellatrix

The same angry, warlike energy currently fused with America's Mars sits on Trump's Sun/North Node in the house of his career. Bellatrix here makes Trump an uber-Mercurial Gemini, giving him his nasty, whip-like tongue, his energy and fighting spirit, but also the reckless aggression of a belligerent daredevil. An empowering tool in his climb to the top, Bellatrix here is one of the many energies that will inevitably lead to his ultimate sudden dishonor and ruin. Whoever rises to the top using the dark energy of Bellatrix pays the price of being forevermore surrounded by enemies and hatred.

Pollux

Termed by the ancients "the wicked Boy", positioned on Trump's Saturn (lessons/karma/blowback) Pollux indicates a brutal, tyrannical, violent, cruel, rash nature, and gives him his love of fighting, malevolence, a foul temper, bitter sarcasm, his brief eminence and renown and the likelihood of a sudden death.

Ras Alhague

Positioned on Trump's Moon (his emotional life/relationships with his mother/women) Ras Alhague brings him his public prominence and gain, as well as his ultimate misfortune through women, his perverted tastes, and mental depravity.

Seginus

On Trump's Jupiter Seginus gives Trump his gift for public speaking, his surly, slippery, crafty mind, his shamelessness, together with losses through his associates and companies.

Pavo

Located on Trump's Vertex, the point in his chart called the degree of fate, all the disaster about to rain down on his head is being activated by this point. Known as "the Peacock", it gives Trump his vanity, love of fame, his gaudy, flashy showmanship.

Regulus

Exactly on Trump's Ascendant (again the way he projects his energy) and his Mars (aggression/combat/war) Regulus here gives Trump his fondness for power and his violent temper. An indicator of trouble, scandal, possible imprisonment and an unhappy death, all his grandiosity and pomposity, his perpetual strutting around, his ridiculous sense of self-importance comes from the influence of Regulus together with Pavo, "the Peacock", on his Vertex. The energy of Regulus on the Ascendant symbolizes a man who constantly demands recognition for his achievements and abilities, who likes to catch others off guard, showing off his supposed superiority. Having no idea what the word 'humble' means, his drives and needs are extreme and overpowering. Regulus here describes Trump as a man totally out of touch with everything except his obsessive drive for adulation, power and the acknowledgement from others of his deluded self-concept of his superiority and authority. Mars in this position will ultimately affect Trump's health, this combination of energies meaning he is likely to die very suddenly from either an assassination attempt, or a heart attack.

Algol

Remember Kathy Griffin's bizarre photo of her holding a mock-up of Trump's bloody, severed head? The fact she chose to do that was no accident. Unless it is successfully integrated and creatively used, the energy Algol is one of the nastiest, most unfortunate, dangerous stars in the entire pantheon, in Trump's case resting exactly on his Midheaven – his most public career point. In Babylonian astrology, Algol was literally the most evil star in the Heavens, known as the 'Demon Star', or the 'Gorgon's Head', the name given Algol in China translating as 'piled up corpses'. Associated with dishonesty and lying, it is frequently found in charts of men and women who have influence over large numbers of people. Placed on the Midheaven, as in the case of Trump, it is said to indicate the probability of death by murder, assassination, or decapitation.

Kathy Griffin. Trump. Algol. The 'Gorgon's head'.

I rest my case.

"His primary rules were: never allow the public to cool off; never admit a fault or wrong; never concede that there may be some good in your enemy; never leave room for alternatives; never accept blame; concentrate on one enemy at a time and blame him for everything that goes wrong; people will believe a big lie sooner than a little one; and if you repeat it frequently enough people will sooner or later believe it."

The U.S. Office of Strategic Services profile of Hitler

"When the President does it that means it's not illegal."

Richard Nixon

"No man has a good enough memory to be a successful liar."

Abraham Lincoln

"There was no collusion with Russia. Everyone knows there was no collusion."

Donald Trump

"Follow the money."

John F. Kennedy

5 WATCH IT COME DOWN

William Lilly and Frau Elsbeth Ebertin, two of the greatest astrologers in history, became famous as a result of predictions they made about the fate of important historical figures and events. Known as the 17th century "English Merlin", Lilly was lionized for his accuracy in foretelling both the Great Fire of London in 1666, and the defeat of King Charles II at the Battle of Naseby and his subsequent beheading. Frau Ebertin rose to prominence following her astonishingly accurate predictions about the manner and date of the execution of Russia's Tsar Nicholas II, and Hitler rise to power.

Having read the countless predictions made by astrologers all over the internet that Hillary Clinton would win the 2016 election in a slam dunk, two and a half years ago, a few months prior to the election, I wrote the following in a post to my followers and friends.

"Contrary to what has been written by the vast majority of astrologers about the 2016 election -- i.e. that Clinton will win, and that Trump hasn't got a hope in hell – the odds are, unfortunately, precisely the opposite. The likelihood of Trump winning is high, if for no other reasons than that the email controversy is not going to go away, and because Trump believes so strongly in the inevitability of his future reality as the President of the United States, and has the arrogance and the ability to sway millions of dissatisfied, disenfranchised primarily white men and women in the rust belt, the midwest and the south whose faith in the American political system has rightly been shot to hell. The only consolation I can offer those who fear for the future of America under Trump is that if he wins, he will barely survive his first term. Before the end of 2020, whether he wins the election or not, Trump will go down like a $20 hooker. It is written in the stars."

Character is destiny. As I explained in the introduction to this book, because Trump is a spiritual Neanderthal who has done zero work in this lifetime to bring his enormous Jungian black shadow bag of psychological darkness to the light, he has no free will whatsoever, hence the inevitability of the blowback from a life wasted in mindless acts of self-aggrandizement, cruelty and greed raining down on his head like a fated ton of lead bricks in 2019, 2020 and beyond, whether he had been elected President, or not.

My words above -- what I sensed months before would be the result of the 2016 election -- were written in response to predictions made by the most popular astrologer in America today and several of her colleagues and friends to illustrate my point about the dangers of what I call the snake oil peddler aspect of the business of astrology.

By her own account Susan Miller has a website that attracts over six million visitors every month, several hundred thousand followers on Twitter, over twenty employees, a lucrative app on iTunes, a personal trainer, a stylist and a publicist. In the many articles that have been written about her she has been named an "elite astrologer", the "reigning queen of astrology", the "go-to astrologer for Emma Stone, Katy Perry, Kirsten Dunst, Cameron Diaz", and "the New York fashion set". With a digital empire worth a small fortune, according to Ms. Miller, 38% of her readers earn over $150,000 a year and are "very educated", 73% having received either college or graduate degrees.

All I can say to that is, if it's true, what damning confirmation it is of the declining standards of the American educational system.

A 2014 article on *New York Magazine's* internet fashion resource, *The Cut*, implied Ms. Miller is a charlatan. While I wouldn't go as far as to state that, having studied her work to my mind she is exploiting people's ignorance for her personal gain under the pretense of assisting them with their lives. She is not deep enough in her knowledge or wisdom to do that, and to my mind does not fundamentally care about the neuroses and problems of the people she addresses in her ludicrous monthly and annual columns and books, using her website and marketing chops to promote herself as a quasi-celebrity guru and master astrologer.

"Trump doesn't have any aspects that could help him get easily into power." "Of all the Republican candidates I feel Scott Walker has the best chance of being nominated for the Republican party." "Rand Paul will definitely be chosen for something in the new administration."

Those are some the predictions Ms. Miller made about the last election.

Forget for a minute how categorically wrong she was about Trump. Scott Walker? Rand Paul? Has anyone heard a significant peep out of either one of them since?

On August 1, 2016, in *The Hollywood Reporter* Ms. Miller dug herself a deeper grave, predicting that Trump would "wobble and won't make it to the election", and that Hillary "has a great chance of becoming President", because "the email scandal isn't resurfacing, and there won't be any others", adding "Hillary's career is at a pinnacle" and "she will likely win, but we won't know for a few days after the election."

Susan Miller, like every one of her colleagues who trumpet their wisdom online while marketing meaningless junk and trivia to their admirers and fans, should stick to her doubtless highly profitable business of pedaling Libra necklaces and Scorpio soap, or better still invest in a crystal ball and a gypsy headscarf, rebranding herself as 'Madam cross my palm with silver for your Pisces 2019 forecast Miller'. A master astrologer she ain't.

If you want the specific timeline of Trump's inevitable decline and fall, here it is.

The same relentless, ruthless astrological powerhouse of the zodiac that will be responsible for bringing America to its knees, spawning its death and rebirth, is the same primary planetary force that will devastate Trump, again no accident given Trump is the man America has chosen to lead the country at the very moment it is heading into its proverbial sunset.

Beginning on January 21, 2019, continuing through 2020 and 2021, Pluto makes a series of shattering, crippling passes back and forth over key points in Trump's chart that will uncover, assault and level to the ground every last vestige of corruption and decay within his rotten, filthy soul. The process begins, however, with a total lunar eclipse.

Eclipses, particularly total eclipses of either the Sun or Moon, trigger unexpected, dramatic changes in the lives of nations and individuals they effect that sometimes occur at the exact time of the eclipse, sometimes weeks or months afterwards. In Trump's case it will be the eclipses of the Sun and Moon between the time of this book's publication and the end of 2020, allied with the ruthless, implacable energy of Pluto stripping away every last vestige of any cover up of the multiple crimes he has committed over the course of his life that will destroy him. And in 2021 and 2022 the disorientation and confusion wrought by the once-in-a-lifetime transit of Neptune besieging his Sun and Moon will be the energies that finish him off.

Things began to get rocky for Trump in August, 2018 during the after burn of the Blood Moon total eclipse of July 27, one of the angriest lunar eclipses of the century, termed a Blood Moon because of the rust red hue imparted to the moon by light refracted from the earth's atmosphere caused by volcanic explosions, pollution and the burning of the Amazon rainforest. The raging energy of this eclipse hitting the area of Trump's chart ruling secrets, self-undoing and hidden enemies, within a month Michael Cohen had surrendered to the FBI, pleading guilty to eight charges, implicating Trump in his plea while not identifying him by name, Cohen's lawyer stating Trump should be prosecuted for the crimes he instructed his client to commit -- on the same day that Paul Manafort was convicted of tax and bank fraud, subsequently agreeing to co-operate with the Special Counsel and his team.

Since the fall of 2018 Trump and his legal team have been dealing with the fall-out from these twin bombshell events, attempting to tap dance their way around questions submitted to them by Mueller regarding the Russian investigation, on November 20, 2018 finally submitting Trump's written answers.

Two weeks before this book's publication Trump lashed out at reporters on the White House lawn in response to questions about a *New York Times* report that the FBI began a probe into him for possible obstruction of justice following his firing of James Comey, Trump's temper exacerbated by news that both current and former U.S. officials had informed *The Washington Post* he had forbidden his translator at a private meeting with Putin at the 2017 G20 summit to share her transcript of what the two men had discussed with his White House aides.

"I never worked for Russia! Not only did I never work for Russia, I think it's a disgrace that you even ask that question!", Trump yelled at the journalists, slamming the FBI officials who launched the probe as "known scoundrels" and "dirty cops" in his inimitable "the lady doth protest too much methinks" Jungian black bag projection fashion.

Meanwhile Trump's former senior campaign aide, Rick Gates, continues to co-operate with Mueller and his team on several ongoing investigations, Trump's nominee for the office of Attorney General, Robert Barr, making it clear he believes it is vitally important Mueller completes his investigation and that the public and Congress be informed of the results.

As I have repeatedly stated in this book, Trump's shocking, ignominious fall is inevitable, and somewhere deep inside him he knows it. In astrological terms the reason it has taken so long for humpty dumpty to fall is because of a temporary fusion of protective energy provided by Venus and Jupiter in his chart, (astrology's two benefic planets). Despite the intensity of the Russia probe, the charges brought against five Americans formerly affiliated with Trump's campaign or administration, thirteen Russian nationals, a dozen Russian intelligence officers and three Russian companies, despite the multiple accusations of sexual harassment, pussy-grabbing and rape levelled against him during the run up to the election, because of the temporary protection of Venus/Jupiter all of the above have bounced off Trump, as if he is wearing an invisible Kevlar jacket. For a short while still it will be the same bullying, braggadocio, nasty business as usual inside the White House, but by February, 2019, as the energy of the Super Blood Wolf Moon total eclipse of January 21 shakes Trump's life to the core and the protection of Venus/Jupiter in his chart begins to wane, a severely rattled Trump will be forced to begin circling his wagons.

Whether it is the revelations delivered in Mueller's report, more bombs dropped by Michael Cohen, or by America Media Inc., the parent company of the *National Enquirer* as a result of its non-prosecution agreement to co-operate with the ongoing investigation into Trump's affairs by the Southern District of New York, or by the nineteen women who have accused Trump of sexual assault and harassment -- not to mention the "Jane Doe" who filed the 2016 lawsuit claiming she was repeatedly raped by Trump at the series of sex parties hosted by Jeffrey Epstein – or a combination of any or all of the above, Trump is done and dusted, the astrological architects of his inevitable oncoming demise the eclipse cycle of 2019 and 2020, Pluto, the lord of destruction, and Neptune, the planet of disorientation and confusion. Even if, as has been predicted by some, the delivery of Mueller's report proves to be an anti-climax, fizzling out like a damp squib on the 4th of July, Trump will be unable to escape his ineluctable destiny.

The Super Blood Wolf Moon total eclipse of January 21, 2019, a fierce astrological event hitting Trump's Saturn, lord of karma and payback, again in his house of secrets, hidden enemies and self-undoing – an eclipse which I have predicted over the coming months will trigger the delivery of Mueller's report – heralded the beginning of Trump's messy, bloody end, his chart on the night of the eclipse showing a man in the grips of a serious depression he has been fighting to conceal since November, 2018, Saturn's tense aspect to his Neptune at the end of the year making him feel one of his most precious ambitions, the wall between the United States and Mexico, is unachievable. The eclipse making a tight, tense aspect to Uranus (sudden, dramatic change), triggering the blowback energy from Saturn, the emotional intensity of the following months will create an energetic cluster-fuck in Trump's life of earth-shattering proportions.

And it just gets worse from there on.

The shit hits the fan big time for Trump in February, 2019, the impact of the eclipse delivering its aftershocks at the same time Saturn attacks Chiron in his chart, his core hidden wound of worthlessness and shame. Saturn's harsh energy hitting the most secret, insecure area of Trump's psyche on and off throughout 2019 will provoke a major crisis in his life, knocking his confidence, creating fears in him that he can't cut the mustard, that he's suddenly not up to the job, that he's somehow lost his precious mojo and can't get it back, that he no longer has the energy or the ability to be effective.

The bruising energy of Saturn attacking Chiron in Trump's chart repeats itself in September and October, the situation ratcheting up in intensity prior to that, during March, April, May and June when, against the backdrop described above Uranus triggers the energy imprint left by the Super Blood Wolf Moon eclipse, making an unpredictable assault on Trump's Saturn in his same house of buried secrets, hidden enemies and self-sabotage, Uranus' sudden, unexpected assault heralding shocking, out of the blue revelations destined to create massive difficulties for him -- health problems, together with a free floating sense of anxiety that will lead to a deepening of what by then will have become Trump's inescapable sense of foreboding, isolation, depression and despair.

To repeat, the same relentless, devastating energy behind the death and rebirth of America – Pluto -- will be the planetary force that brings Trump to his knees. In earlier chapters I explained the profound function and energy of Pluto with regard to America's destiny. The same applies to Trump – except that in his case there will be no rebirth. He's too far gone. It's too late. For Trump -- the fat boy -- the fat lady has sung.

Pluto annihilates everything impure and defiled in a person or nation, raising it to the ground in order to rebirth it at a higher level, hence Pluto and Scorpio's symbol of the phoenix rising from the ashes of its former self. In Trump's chart as I write this Pluto is relentlessly ploughing through his house of children, sex and love affairs, rapidly approaching its deeply fated, once-in-a-lifetime, shattering encounter with Planet, the planet of blowback and karma in the 11th house of his social standing, ultimate goals and friends.

Because of Pluto's protracted 248-year orbit around the zodiac, the transit of the lord of death and rebirth opposite Saturn thankfully can happen only once in anyone's lifetime. I say thankfully because the protracted collision of Pluto with Saturn is without question one of the most gruesome, relentless, depressing experiences any human being can go through, anyone walking through that time forced to batten down the hatches and hang on for dear life through a seemingly never-ending assault of furious, raging energy relentlessly attacking every corrupt area of their lives they previously believed to be secure and unassailable. The classic irresistible force meets an immovable object experience, in Trump's case it will manifest as the most brutal challenge he has ever faced in his life, because of the level of corruption in his soul, and the nature of the crimes he has committed, an experience that will quite simply destroy him.

Several of the most intense moments of Trump's encounter with Pluto assailing his Saturn hit him as soon as March, 2019, repeating in December and January, February and March, 2020, repeating again from August, 2020 through to the end of the year, in February, 2019 Pluto making its first pass over his Vertex, the fated degree of the zodiac known as destiny's gate, the only point in the chart responsible for fated encounters and events, in Trump's case located in his 5th house of children, sex and love affairs, directly opposing his Saturn, signifying a major event, or series of events involving and/or precipitated by the actions of one or more of his children and his past sexual encounters that will lead to the deepening of his social ostracism.

Trump's isolation inside the White House over the Christmas holidays of 2019/2020 was a taste of things to come. Like Macbeth isolated in his castle, friendless and alone as he approaches his brutal, bloody end, as we move through 2019 and into 2020 Trump will find himself the subject of increasing judgment, abandoned and alone, the protracted, once in a lifetime transit of Pluto opposite his natal Saturn the final nail in his proverbial coffin. As I wrote in my post two and a half years ago, Trump will be lucky to survive his first term, and with Neptune (disillusionment/abandonment), the natural ruler of the house of incarceration and banishment making its once in a lifetime attack on both his Sun and his Moon (Trump's ego and his emotions/relationships with women) for three years from February, 2020 to February, 2023, it is my belief that Trump, together with Don Jr. and Jared Kushner will wind up behind bars. Whether or not he is impeached, jailed, or both, there is no question that by this time Trump will have be in the grips of a crushing identity crisis, his career in ruins, the façade of his marriage exposed, the combined transformative forces of Pluto, Saturn and Neptune having performed their collective task on behalf of the universe perfectly.

"Bohm and Pribram's theories provide a profound new way of looking at the world. Our brains construct objective reality by interpreting projections from another dimension, a deeper order of existence beyond space and time. The brain is a hologram enfolded in a holographic universe."

Michael Talbot, *The Holographic Universe*

"It is hard to recognize that thought and belief combine into a power surge that can literally move mountains."

Jesus Christ, *A Course In Miracles*

"You are given the gift of the gods. You create your reality according to your beliefs."

Jane Roberts, *The Nature of Personal Reality*

"The human mind *is* the universe. What is light without an eye to see it?"

Alan Watts

6 THE COSMOCENTRIC REVOLUTION

In 1991 a groundbreaking book on the profound implications of a series of astonishing discoveries in quantum physics and the paranormal was published. Written by a man named Michael Talbot, *The Holographic Universe* was a thrilling exploration of the nature of human consciousness and the universe. Throwing down the gauntlet to contemporary science, Talbot challenged the perception of physical reality that has dominated human thought for thousands of years with the stunning proposition that what we perceive as objective reality is an illusion, and that the universe is in fact a hologram.

Beginning with the retelling of one of the 20th century's most famous scientific experiments in which the French quantum physicist Alain Aspect proved the ability of subatomic particles (which make up more than 99.9% of the human body) to communicate with each other instantaneously whether they are 10 feet, or 10 billion miles apart, a conclusion violating a fundamental law of modern physics -- Einstein's tenet that no communication can travel faster than the speed of light -- Talbot unveiled his tantalizing proposition that the universe as we have hitherto understood it does not exist.

The success of Aspect's experiment supported the findings of two brilliant maverick scientists working in independent fields on opposite sides of the Atlantic – Einstein's protégé, the theoretical physicist David Bohm, and the Stanford based neurophysiologist Karl Pribram -- both of whom had separately arrived at the same conclusion about the holographic nature of the universe and human reality, Bohm believing the reason subatomic particles can communicate over such vast distances is that their separateness is an illusion, that at a fundamental level the particles are not individual entities, but extensions of the same universal energy – Pribram's conclusion being that because the brain functions holographically there is no such thing as objective reality, what we perceive as reality being nothing more than an illusion we construct inside our minds.

The implications of the holographic nature of the universe are legion, radical and monumental, not the least of which are the following -- that there is no 'out there' out there; that, as Einstein believed, the past, present and future co-exist; that telepathy and psychic knowing involve the ability to access the vast field of infinite probabilities contained within the gigantic cosmic hologram; and that, whether we choose to acknowledge it or not, we are 100%, 24/7 the creators of our own reality.

While these are some of the most astonishing conclusions drawn from the holographic model of the universe, others equally breathtaking and dramatic have resulted from investigations undertaken by individuals such as Talbot, myself and others into the subjects of reincarnation, life after death, miraculous healing, and man's relationship to God.

While my own adventures and experiences in these realms will be the subject of another book, Michael Talbot's earlier work *Your Past Lives, A Reincarnation Handbook,* is an invaluable guidebook that explains various techniques that can be used to explore one's past lives, a book on a par with Brian Weiss's, *Many Lives, Many Masters,* which I also recommend.

In his investigations into the Near Death Experience Talbot noted many people recalled the same memory of not having a body unless they were "thinking", and that as their experience of the between-life state continued they gradually became a kind of "hologram-like composite of all their former selves", the composite having a different name from any of the names they had used in any of their remembered physical incarnations.

With regard to miraculous healing, Talbot cited several instances that confirm the holographic model of reality and the physical universe, the most remarkable being the stories of a sixteen year-old boy diagnosed with an advanced case of Brocq's disease, and a man who in 1957 found himself at death's door with a case of malignant lymphoma, both diseases to this day believed by the medical establishment to be incurable.

A horribly disfiguring, hereditary condition, victims of Brocq's disease develop a thick, horny covering over their skin resembling the scales of a reptile. With the disease at its most advanced, gruesome stage, as a last resort the boy was referred to a hypnotherapist. Finding the boy a good subject, easily put into a deep trance, during the course of his first appointment the hypnotherapist was able to convince the boy's unconscious mind that his disease was healing and would soon be gone. Five days later the scaly layer covering the boy's left arm fell off, revealing soft, healthy flesh beneath. Ten days later his arm was completely normal.

The hypnotherapist continued to work on different areas of the boy's body until every piece of the scaly skin was gone. The boy remained symptom free the next five years, at which point the hypnotherapist lost touch with him.

The fact that Brocq's disease is a genetic condition made the boy's total recovery all the more startling, the takeaway being that once we access the deepest strata of our beliefs, our consciousness is so powerful it can literally alter our DNA.

The details of the case of the man with advanced, malignant lymphoma was similarly extraordinary. Bedridden, feverish, gasping for air, his body riddled with massive tumors, fluid filling his chest having to be removed every two days, when the man overheard a discussion about a new cancer cure serum being tested in the hospital he begged his doctor to be given the drug. What did he have to lose? His doctor agreeing, the drug was duly administered.

The patient's recovery was to startling. Within three days the man was out of his hospital bed, striding down the halls of his ward, flirting with the nurses, x-rays showing his tumors once the size of oranges had shrunk to the size of golf balls. Ten days later he was discharged from the hospital, cancer-free.

Two months passed, the patient remaining in the pink of health. Then reports came out that the trial drug he had been administered had been concluded to be worthless. Within days the man's tumors returned and he was back in hospital, bedridden, staring death in the face once again.

Sensing his patient's mind had somehow been involved in the rapid changes in the man's condition, his doctor decided to take a radical step that today would be considered totally unethical.

He lied.

The reports he had heard about the drug, the doctor told the man, were wrong. The serum he had been administered had been proven to be a highly potent and effective miracle cancer cure. Asked by his patient why, if this was the case, he had suffered a relapse, the doctor told the man he had been given a dose from a weak batch. The hospital was expecting a new shipment twice the strength by the end of the week.

Three days later the doctor rolled up his patient's sleeve, administering another injection into his arm – of spring water.

Again the patient's tumors shrank, all other symptoms of his cancer magically disappearing. Within a week, no further trace of his tumors found in his body, he was once again declared cancer free and released from hospital

Living happily for over two months without any form of relapse, the American Medical Association released a final report issuing its conclusive verdict on the cancer drug, declaring it useless. The man's tumors and all of his other symptoms immediately returned. This time, two days after being readmitted to the hospital, he was dead.

Both these stories echoed my own experience of miraculous healing that occurred ten years ago when I developed a case of ulcerative colitis at the 9 out of 10 critical stage. A deeply unpleasant, excruciating condition related to Crohn's disease, Hashimoto's syndrome and Grave's disease, all conditions deemed incurable by medicine, doctors taught in medical school that any pathology of the central immune system means one thing – a very expensive course of barely effective medication with nasty side effects lasting the rest of the patient's life -- knowing this could not be true, that nothing is incurable, I refused to experience the pleasure of having my colon removed for the price of $100,000, instead choosing to go down on my knees in a park, tears streaming down my face as I prayed to be given the answer by the good Lord. Thirty minutes later I received that answer, three months later, thanks to my grit and faith together with massive doses of aloe vera taken internally provided by a product called *Digestacure*, a naturopathic remedy for diseases of the central immune system that still to this day has not been approved by the FDA, finding myself symptom free. I have remained so ever since.

Talbot's research into the God experience centered around the work of Emmanuel Swedenborg, the 18th century philosopher, theologian, scientist, visionary and mystic whose best known work was his book on the afterlife, *Heaven and Hell*. Swedenborg was another polymath genius, ahead of his time. The first man in science to anticipate the existence of the neuron, gifted with stunningly accurate insights into the structure and functioning of the brain, the nervous system and the pituitary gland, it was in the world of metaphysics that Swedenborg was destined to make his biggest mark.

A natural mystic, determined to understand the order and purpose of creation and to discover how matter relates to spirit, in both *Heaven and Hell* and other works Swedenborg described his detailed visions of the afterlife and his interactions with spirit beings and deceased human beings that dwell there, his ultimate perspective on God, creation and the relationship between God and man remarkably similar to those conclusions drawn by Pribram, Bohm, Talbot, myself and others about the holographic nature of the universe.

Describing every human being as "a heaven in miniature", words that echo the holographic principle that the whole is the part, and the part is the whole, one of the central tenets of Swedenborg's belief system was that everything that exists has a correspondence with things that exist in the spirit world, and that everything we see in objective reality is a portrayal of a deeper reality.

"Further, in regard to the union of Heaven with the human race, it should be realized that the Lord himself is flowing into every individual according to Heaven's design – into the individual's most inward and most outward aspects alike", Swedenborg wrote in *Heaven and Hell*.

Talbot's research into reincarnation, the Near Death Experience, miraculous healings, and the God experience via his study of the work of Swedenborg echoed the most stunning aspect of the conclusion drawn separately by Pribram and Bohm about the holographic nature of the universe and the human brain when put together – that the concrete nature of the world around us is a slight of hand, a cosmic trick, an illusion which according to our beliefs and expectations we are unconsciously constantly hypnotizing ourselves into manifesting, plucking from the vast cosmic soup of infinite probabilities contained within the gigantic super-hologram in which our existence is couched – what Bohm referred to as the 'implicate order'.

It also replicated what Talbot had read years earlier in his study of the work of the remarkable, but little known American writer, poet and psychic, Jane Roberts, the trance channel for an "energy personality essence no longer focused in physical reality" named Seth.

"To my great surprise and slight annoyance, I found Seth eloquently and lucidly articulated a view of reality I had arrived at only after great effort, and an extensive study of both paranormal phenomena and quantum physics", wrote Talbot in his earlier book, *Beyond the Quantum*.

Fifty-five years ago Jane Roberts began an extraordinary journey of self-discovery, her self-described "adventures in consciousness", a series of transcendental experiences that culminated in the production of a book of automatic writing. In the course of an after dinner poetry writing session, Jane felt her consciousness leave her body, her mind suddenly barraged with ideas that were astonishing and new to her.

"It was very domestic, very normal, very unpsychedelic," she later remembered. "Then, between one normal minute and the next, a fantastic avalanche of radical, new ideas burst into my head with tremendous force. It was as if the physical world was really tissue-paper-thin, hiding infinite dimensions of reality, and I was flung through the tissue paper with a huge ripping sound."

When she returned to consciousness Jane found herself scribbling down the title for a batch of notes she had written while in an apparently altered state, *The Physical Universe As Idea Construction.*

Thus began Jane Roberts' twenty-one years of experience as a trance channel for Seth, an aspect of her higher self, in the course of which she wrote over twenty books either dictated by and/or related to Seth's teachings, plus another six dealing with the subject of life after death, three of which expressed what Jane termed as the "after death world views" of noted individuals in philosophy and art, ranging from the 19th century American philosopher William James, to the painters Rembrandt and Paul Cezanne.

As Talbot noted, the core tenets of Seth's teachings are identical to the implications of the holographic model of the universe -- that all time is simultaneous; that we are here to learn the responsibility for creating our reality through our thoughts, expectations, and beliefs; that human existence is couched in a vast sea of infinite probabilities.

The work of Jane Roberts is intimately connected to the 19th. century New Thought Movement and the teachings of Christian Science championed by thinkers such as Mary Baker Eddy, William James, and Phineas Quimby, as well as linked to writers such as Napoleon Hill, whose classic work on the power of the human mind, *Think and Grow Rich* was ranked number two on a list compiled by *The Christian Science Monitor* of the top ten most influential, best-selling self-help books of all time.

The impact of Jane's body of work on writers and thinkers in today's New Age movement has been more profound than any other, the jacket of one of her first Seth books, *The Nature of Personal Reality*, bearing testimonials from Deepak Choprah, Marianne Williamson, Louise Hay, Dan Millman, Richard Bach and many others, each declaring the enormous influence Seth had on their awakening. The debt of gratitude owed Jane by every teacher of the power of the human mind today -- from Esther Hicks, to Anthony Robbins, to Rhonda Byrne, the producer of *The Secret*, and every individual who has built their reputations as teachers of The Law of Attraction from their participation in Byrne's DVD -- is incalculable, *The Law of Attraction* and *The Secret* being nothing more than highly-commercialized, glammed-up, coffee table versions of Jane's teachings for the masses. *The Collected Works of Jane Roberts and Seth For Dummies.*

The work of Jane Roberts together with the discoveries about the holographic nature of the universe described in Michael Talbot's book lie at the heart of ***The Cosmocentric Revolution***. These individuals are giants, champions in the field of the human adventure, each one of them playing their vital part in the salvation of the planet and the renaissance of the human spirit we are so desperately seeking now. They stand on the shoulders of the countless great philosophers, writers and thinkers who have gone before them -- Goethe, Spinoza, Descartes, Rousseau, Voltaire, Montesquieu, Immanuel Kant, Swedenborg, David Hume, Adam Smith, Locke, and the founding fathers they inspired in the writing of the *Declaration of Independence, the United States Constitution*, and the *Bill of Rights* – George Washington, James Madison, Benjamin Franklin, Thomas Jefferson, Thomas Paine, John Adams and the greatest, most eloquent, literate President in the history of the United States of America, John F. Kennedy.

If you want to change the world – if you wish to alter any aspect of your experience, either personal or global, you must begin by examining your expectations and beliefs, consciously changing every negative thought you have allowed to dominate your mind to its opposite. Your body, your life and the world you see around you are perfect mirrors of your mind, the outward portrait of an inward condition. Reflections of your beliefs – conscious and hidden. Change your mind, and you will change your world. To repeat my words from the introduction, this ability to master your mind, learning to become a conscious co-creator with the source of All That Is – is the reason you are here.

The quicker you embrace this truth – the faster you become aware of your conscious and unconscious expectations, thoughts, desires and beliefs, disciplining your mind, erasing every negative, fearful lie coming from the limited concept of your mind, the sorry, little 'I' of your ego, replacing them with their diametric opposites, the more dramatically, dynamically and rapidly your life and the world around you will change. It is called mastery. It is called oneness with God. And like every beautiful and powerful thing in this world, once learned, it is child's play.

"Our world and everything in it – from snowflakes to maple trees, to falling stars and spinning electrons – are only ghostly images, projections from a level of reality so beyond our own that it is literally beyond both space and time", wrote Michael Talbot at the conclusion of *The Holographic Universe*.

In a holographic universe there are no limits to the extent to which you can alter the fabric of reality, for what you perceive as reality is merely a blank canvas waiting for you to draw on it any future you want.

In a holographic universe magic is your divine birthright.

"All probable worlds exist now. All probable variations on the most minute aspect of any reality exist now. You weave in and out of probabilities constantly, picking and choosing as you go along."

Jane Roberts, *The Nature of Personal Reality*

"Your mind creates the future and will turn it back to full creation any moment."

Jesus Christ, *A Course in Miracles*

"People like us, who believe in physics, know that the distinction between the past, present and future is only a stubbornly persistent illusion."

Albert Einstein

"You wander from room to room, hunting for the diamond necklace that is already around your neck."

Rumi

7 WHICH YOU? WHICH WORLD?

"When it is dark enough, you can see the stars." Those words written by the great 19th century American poet and philosopher, the leader of the transcendentalist movement, Ralph Waldo Emerson, offer us a sense of hope at a time when darkness seems to be more pervasive in this world than ever.

Emerson was a pantheist. He believed that God is everywhere, that God exists in all things. He believed, as I do, that all of reality is identical with Divinity. He understood that man is a portion of God and that God is the source of all things.

In other words, he understood that the universe is a hologram.

One of the most radical, mind-bending concepts in the work of Jane Roberts is the concept of probable future realities and probable selves. The bedrock of Jane's teachings is not only that we are responsible for creating our own reality, but that both the universe and our personal reality are far more creative and plastic than we have hitherto supposed – that at the deepest level of reality we exist as probable versions of ourselves constantly weaving in and out of an infinite variety of probable futures and probable future worlds.

Mainstream science shuffles cautiously along at a snail's pace, the vast majority of scientists terrified of becoming a Copernicus or a Galileo, of losing their precious salaries and tenured professorships should, God forbid, they risk going out on a limb to declare any radical new theory the truth. That is why, despite its acknowledgement by mainstream scientists such as David Bohm and Stephen Hawking, the Many-Worlds Theory, the hypothesis that an infinite number of universes exist in which the past and the present, together with everything that could happen in the future, or could have happened in the past is the true nature of reality for the present remains in the realms of *Star Trek* and *Stranger Things* – science fiction fantasy.

As I have emphasized in this book, the monumental transformation of consciousness we are in the midst of – the earth-shattering paradigm shift in our understanding of who and what we are, the nature of the universe and human reality I term **The Cosmocentric Revolution** – will ultimately be remembered as the most profound, important paradigm shift in human history. At the core of this revolution are the stunning insights mentioned in the previous chapter, logical conclusions that stem from the understanding that the universe is a hologram -- that there is no 'out there' out there; that, as Einstein believed, the past, present, and future simultaneously co-exist; that telepathy and psychic knowing involve the ability to access the vast field of infinite probabilities within the giant cosmic hologram; and that, whether we choose to acknowledge it or not, we are 100%, 24/7 the creators of our own reality. These are the truths that rest at the heart of **The Cosmocentric Revolution**. But by far the most important of these are the recognition of the simultaneous nature of time, and the fact that we have the freedom, the power, and the responsibility for creating our future.

Fifty-eight years ago the greatest President in the history of the United States was sworn into office. The 35th President, John F. Kennedy, was an outstanding example of the highest qualities in humanity, blessed to be born with all the glorious gifts of the fixed star Aldebaran conjunct his Sun, the star of Archangel Michael, the commander of the Heavenly Host -- honor, intelligence, eloquence, integrity, steadfastness, popularity and courage – qualities exemplified and amplified by his energy and presence. In his all too brief life on this earth, John F. Kennedy was the light of the world.

On November 22, 1963 Kennedy was assassinated at the behest of a covert group of special interest groups IN the American secret government headed by Allen Dulles, James Jesus Angleton of the CIA, and the military-industrial complex, primarily for one reason – that Kennedy was determined to halt the American war machine and usher in an age of peace.

His life tragically cut short a year before the end of his first term of office, Kennedy's legacy was nonetheless extraordinary. Indeed, given the phenomenal pressures exerted on him from every quarter – not the least of which were the aggressiveness of the CIA and the Pentagon – the list of his achievements, together with what he would have gone on to accomplish had he been permitted to live, is nothing less than phenomenal.

A little more than two years prior to his assassination, in September, 1961, Kennedy delivered a keynote address at the United Nations General Assembly in New York.

"Never before has man had such capacity to control his environment, to end thirst and hunger, to conquer poverty and disease, to banish illiteracy and human misery. We have the power to make this the best generation of mankind in the history of the world -- or to make it the last. Today, every inhabitant of this planet must contemplate the day when this planet may no longer be habitable. Every man, woman and child lives under a nuclear sword of Damocles, hanging by the slenderest of threads, capable of being cut at any moment by accident or miscalculation, or by madness. The weapons of war must be abolished before they abolish us. Ladies and gentlemen of this Assembly, the decision is ours. Never have the nations of the world had so much to lose, or so much to gain. Together we shall save our planet, or together we shall perish in its flames. Save it we can, and save it we must. Then shall we earn the eternal thanks of mankind and, as peacemakers, the eternal blessing of God."

Kennedy's words echoed the thoughts of another of America's greatest Presidents, Abraham Lincoln, when he said, "My dream is of a place and a time where America will once again be seen as the last best hope on earth."

There is no doubt that had Kennedy lived, America and the world you and I are living in would have been astonishingly different.

That vision of America and the world, the vision of Kennedy, Lincoln, and the Founding Fathers still exists in the collective mythic imagination, in a different probable reality. The America and the world in that reality are an America and a world of enlightenment, prosperity, harmony, peace and love – a world of unilateral disarmament, in which the American war machine has been halted, a world where the population levels of the earth have been peacefully, healthily, consciously brought under control, a world in which the pollution of the earth's environment is no longer a problem, limitless, renewable energy sources discovered and made available to all, a world in which every disease previously believed to be incurable has been eradicated.

To repeat, the probable reality of that America and that world exists. Now.

A long time ago I predicted the salvation of America will come from the rise of African-American and ethnic minority women in American politics -- having drawn her chart from the information I received from her campaign manager, an energy healer, projecting the victory of Alexandria Ocasio-Cortez in New York's 14th congressional district, the biggest upset in the 2018 mid-terms, and that within the next twelve years Alexandria Ocasio-Cortez will be sitting behind the Resolute desk inside the Oval Office.

Alexandria Ocasio-Cortez, a Bronx born woman of Puerto Rican descent; Ilhan Omar, a Muslin woman born in Somalia; Rashaida Tlaib, the Detroit born daughter of Palestinian immigrants, and another Muslim; the Samoan born Hindu Senator for Hawaii, Tulsi Gabbar; the Californian Senator Kamala Harris, the daughter of immigrant parents from Jamaica and India, and Ayanna Pressley are examples of these ethnic minority and African-American women whose inevitable rise to power I have predicted. These women are the future leaders of the America that will emerge on the probable future timeline of the healed nation as it completes its dark night of the soul, emerging into the light of a bright and brilliant, brand new day. The fact that they are here now in our current reality, rising fiercely to power, pushing back against the darkness of Trump and the Republican party is a sign we are on the right path – that the probable future timeline of America's bright and brilliant brand new day is on our collective horizon.

The platforms these women are standing on, the issues they are fighting for -- from abortion rights to gun control, from the legalization of marijuana to LGBT rights, from immigration to healthcare, from the abolition of the death penalty to the solution of the critical environmental issues of global warming and the plastic polluting the world's oceans herald the emergence of the reborn America and world envisioned by Kennedy, Lincoln, and the Founding Fathers.

"These are the times that try men's souls", wrote the Founding Father Thomas Paine in *The American Crisis*. "If there must be trouble, let it be in my day, that my child may have peace. Those who expect to reap the blessings of freedom must, like men, undergo the fatigue of supporting it."

Taking action, standing up and being counted, supporting these women and the others like them who will emerge onto the political scene during the following five years is critical. Action you take in the physical world will play as crucial a part in the creation of the brave new America and the brave new world as the information that follows below. Yet that information and the action you take upon it will be as crucial to your success in support of the biggest transformation of consciousness in human history as any action you take in the outer world, and will be the source of it.

Your point of power is always in the present. You rule your future and your world, individually and collectively, from the limitless power available to you in this moment. Here, right now, wherever you find yourself, you are the creator of **your** own reality, the creator of your future, and your world. If every reader of this book makes the conscious commitment to reprogram their expectations and beliefs, replacing them with the most powerful, vigorous vision they can muster of mankind, America's, and their own future, that future, that America, and that world **_will come to pass_**.

This is not Pollyanna nonsense. It is scientific fact.

This is the heart and soul of *The Cosmocentric Revolution.*

As Jane Roberts taught, we unconsciously weave in and out of our future probabilities effortlessly. Every thought, every beat of your heart is an action imprinting your desire for a certain future reality on the blank slate of the universe, whether conscious, or unconscious. Contrary to what traditional astrology teaches, the future is open ended. Unless you insist on remaining unconscious, at no point in time is any experience predestined. Indeed, there should be no such word in the human lexicon. Contrary to the ancient Arabic concept, *Al-maktoob*, 'that which is written', once you come to consciousness **_nothing has been predetermined_**. Instead you find out you are living in a thrillingly alive universe of infinite probabilities; a universe infinitely more mystical and powerful than you have heretofore understood; a universe in which literally anything you can imagine can be made manifest; a universe in which you stand at the very center – hence the name *The Cosmocentric Revolution*, and hence the vital necessity that you now wake up.

"The message becomes increasingly clear", wrote Michael Talbot at the conclusion of *The Holographic Universe*", "the deeper and more emotionally charged our beliefs, the greater the changes we can make in both our bodies and in reality itself."

It is the intensity of emotion, the passion and the discipline with which you consciously focus your mind on the probable future you desire to exist that will pull that probable future to you. Your mind, the awesome power of the Holy Spirit within you, knows precisely how to do this, and if you get quiet enough, making a dedicated, conscious daily and nightly practice out of this exercise in which you deliberately, intently, powerfully pull that probable future you wish to manifest into being, *it will come to pass*.

There is no time. The future you want has already happened. All you have to do is pull it towards you with your white-hot, laser-focused passion, intensity and belief. The most exalted, powerful probable future you is reaching back in time right now to help you make the right choices and decisions to <u>become</u> that future you, living in that ideal future America and ideal probable future world. The future is nowhere fixed. There are countless roads around you leading to that ideal future world open and available to you in every situation, no matter how dark and depressing your circumstances.

Again, ***this is not Pollyanna nonsense. It is scientific fact,*** and shall be proven so before the time comes for you to depart this earth.

"It seems as if the world determines what you perceive. Instead it is your thoughts that determine the world you see", wrote Jane Roberts in *The Nature of Personal Reality*. "You still think the interior world is symbolic and that the exterior world is real. If you do not like the state of your world, it is you yourselves that must change, individually and en-masse. This is the only way change will be effected. Your events, lives and experiences are caused by your expectations and beliefs. Change the beliefs, and your life will change. The story of your life is written by you. You are its author. There is no reason to view any drama you have unconsciously created as real and believe that you are trapped by it. The power to change every condition of your life is yours. Right here. Right now. You have only to exercise it."

If you have truly grasped and understood the limitless power of your mind, that you truly are the creator of your own reality, at all times and under every circumstance, if you have the serious intent to change your future by consciously assuming the responsibility of altering your expectations and beliefs, then the atmosphere will automatically be created in which the desired changes will occur.

Again, from *The Nature of Personal Reality*, "We are spirits who express ourselves through the miraculous joy of the flesh, who wear as our badge of identity joy and exultation. How many of you would want to limit your reality, your entire reality, to the experience you know now? You do this whenever you imagine what you recognize as yourself is your entire personality, or insist your identity be maintained unchanged through an endless eternity. You must stretch your imagination, rouse yourself from mental lethargy, and be bold enough to discard the limiting, dogmatic comfort blankets of everything you have hitherto believed."

The body appears permanent from one moment to the next, but like the future you and your future world, it constantly dies and is reborn, rising again and again out of the limitless cosmic soup of infinite probabilities according to your expectations, desires and beliefs.

No situation, no condition is permanent. To imagine otherwise is to become hypnotized by your self-created physical symbols. The path of experience is nowhere settled. There is no one road that does not have avenues leading to another. There are deep veins of probable actions, infinite alternate probable futures available to you at all times. There is no world. The walls of your house do not actually exist, so the divisions of time you have artificially decided to place within the present moment, divisions between the past, the present and future, do not exist.

The highest possible future you, the perfect America and the perfect world exist right now in the mythic imagination, reaching out to you, calling out to you, waiting for you to seize them and draw them to you by the power and passion of your intent.

The legendary British mathematician, Andrew Wiles, once described his experience of doggedly pursuing the proof of a radical new mathematical theorem.

"It's like entering a dark mansion", he wrote. "You go into the first room and it's dark, completely dark. You stumble around, bumping into the furniture. Gradually, you learn where each piece of furniture is. Finally, you find the light switch and turn it on. Suddenly the whole house is illuminated, and you can see exactly where you are and where you have been."

This sudden illumination, this "euraka!" moment is what occurs once Michael Talbot's explanation of the work of David Bohm and Karl Pribram in their discovery of the holographic nature of the universe and our human reality is elided with the wisdom contained in the writings of Jane Roberts.

"Who would attempt to fly with the tiny wings of a sparrow when the mighty power of an eagle has been given him?", writes Jesus in *A Course in Miracles*. "All power in earth and Heaven has been given unto you. There is nothing your Holiness cannot do." These words echo the truth spoken by Seth through Jane.

"You are in physical existence to learn and understand that your energy, translated into feelings, thoughts and emotions, causes <u>all</u> experience. <u>There are no exceptions</u>. You get what you concentrate on. You get what you believe. There is no other main rule."

<u>You</u> are the light of the world.

Amen.

"It would never come into their heads to fabricate colossal untruths, and they would not believe others could have the impudence to distort the truth so infamously. Even though the facts which prove this to be so may be brought clearly to their minds, they will still doubt and waver and will continue to think that there may be some other explanation."

Adolf Hitler, *Mein Kampf*

"The majority of politicians are interested not in truth, but in power, and in the maintenance of that power. To maintain that power it is essential that people remain in ignorance; that they live in ignorance of the truth, even the truth of their own lives. What surrounds us, therefore, is a vast tapestry of lies on which we feed."

Harold Pinter, *Nobel Prize Acceptance Speech*

"If you shut up truth and bury it under the ground, it will grow and gather to itself such explosive power that the day it bursts forth, it will blow up everything in its way.

Emile Zola

"Sarah, if the American people ever found out what we've done, they'd chase us down the streets and lynch us."

George H. W. Bush

8 EPILOGUE – THE TRUTH WILL OUT

Referring to observations he made about the state of America following the events of 9/11 and the beginning of the War on Terror, the master of British espionage novels, John Le Carré remarked, "the lies that have been distributed are so many and so persistent, arguably fiction is the only way to tell the truth."

Later in 2019 I am publishing a novel called *Cabal*. A geopolitical thriller for our times dealing with the monumental themes of this book, the heroine of *Cabal*, Julia Logan, is a brilliant, fiercely driven adversarial journalist and documentary film-maker inspired by Laura Poitras, the producer and director of the award winning film on Ed Snowden, *Citizen Four*. In *Cabal* Julia learns the meaning of the phrase 'careful what you wish for' when she makes the mistake of taking the bait offered her by a notorious black hat hacker and a retired CIA officer and former U.S. Navy Colonel, finding herself sucked down a rabbit hole of surreal, terrifying dimensions, a rabbit-hole all the more shocking because it is the rabbit-hole of truth.

At the start of *Cabal*, Julia flies to America from her home in Paris to receive an award for her latest documentary on 9/11 and the Iraq war, a film titled *Total War; Rampant Greed*, and to deliver a talk at TED 2020. The tone and content of Julia's TED talk are exactly like Julia; provocative, incisive, brutally honest and daring, a talk that leaves her audience speechless, not just because of its brilliance, but because in the speech she confronts her audience with the heinous, diabolical truth about the events of 9/11 and the War on Terror. What follows is an extract from the chapter in *Cabal* in which Julia delivers her TED talk. A taste of things to come.

****

Julia stood front stage center on the main stage of the convention center waiting for the applause to die down. As a respectful silence fell over the auditorium, she took a moment to gather her thoughts, then spoke.

"Good afternoon. Welcome to TED, 2020. The title of this talk is *Murder, Inc.*"

She paused, surveying the audience in front of her as the poster for *Total War, Rampant Greed,* appeared on the screen behind her. The mutilated corpse of an American soldier lying in a pool of blood, a photo of Dick Cheney, his feet propped up on a desk, watching the Twin Towers burning on a television screen beside it.

"This year's TED conference is about the search for deeper meaning. In the wake of the political and technological turmoil of the past few years, where are we going? What ideals are truly worth fighting for? This talk stands apart from the other talks on the program, because it is not a talk about the exploration of superhuman new technologies that evoke wonder and awe, nor is it a talk about mind-bending science that will drive the future. Instead this talk is a passionate call to arms – a call to action on the two most critical issues dominating the world today – issues which if we fail to successfully address I and many others believe will signal the death knell for the human race and all life on this planet forever. This is your wake up call to the truth."

The poster for Julia's film wiped to an image of the Twin Towers of the World Trade Center imploding, dissolving into dust.

"9/11 had a devastating impact on the entire world. What I am most concerned with, and what I have attempted to document in my film, *Total War, Rampant Greed,* is precisely what resulted from the U.S. government's fiercely jingoistic response to 9/11; not just the carnage and bloodshed of the War on Terror, but all of the consequences, all of the blowback, the knock-on effects; the erosion of civil liberties in America; the implementation of what has become, despite the courageous revelations of Edward Snowden, an accepted system of illegal mass surveillance; the wholesale adoption of policies of torture, etc."

She turned and looked up at the screen. The image of Cheney wiped to a picture of an American soldier sitting cross-legged on the sands of Iraq, a dead Iraqi infant cradled in his arms.

"Today is the seventeenth anniversary of the beginning of the Iraq War. In this talk I am going to focus on the results of that war. What was achieved, what the cost has been in terms of both human lives and suffering, as well as cold, hard cash. What were the gains, and on the behalf of whom. During this talk you are going to be shown a series of stills from my film. The odds are you will find them disturbing. If that is the case, I shall be happy. I shall be happy, because I shall know that I've done my job. It's time we took the blinkers off. It's time we opened up our eyes and looked at the truth."

The image on the screen wiped to a photo of a Millennial in a skimpy bikini shooting a selfie on her iPhone, a shot of Kim Kardashian wearing the identical bikini beside it.

"One of our biggest problems today, because our lives have become so stressful, because we have become conditioned to believe we all deserve to be multi-millionaires, leading a cushy, jet-set lifestyle, because the majority of us own smart phones and are constantly bombarded with information – most of which is mindless, trivial and utterly meaningless, is that we've given up. We don't want to be bothered with the truth – particularly if that truth is uncomfortable and disturbing. If the truth is too dark, too hard to swallow, the majority of us don't have the time. We simply don't want to know."

The image of the Millennial dissolved to a split screen of four images – a starving polar bear in the Arctic; dead pilot whales washed up on a beach in New Zealand; the Great Pacific Plastic Patch; a dead sea bird, its stomach cut open, revealing the plastic waste the bird had swallowed that killed it.

"That has to change. And it has to change now. If it doesn't, it is my contention, and the contention of countless other men and women like me, that humanity and the natural world are not going to make it. Quite simply we are not going to be here much longer. Make no mistake about it, life as we know it on earth is under assault — from ourselves. And if we don't dial it back, if we don't change, if we don't put an end to the pollution, to our psychopathic passive acceptance of a state of endless global war, as a species we are going to self-destruct, taking the planet and all of its God-given, beautiful, richly diverse wildlife and ecology with us."

The image on the screen wiped to a quote from Julia's film.

'If the earth's environment implodes under the weight of civilization, if we continue to tear each other apart, if we fail to respect the animals and the state of the earth, mankind is doomed.'

Julia turned and looked up at the screen again as it went dark, supplanted moments later by a photo of a little Iraqi girl alone on a desert road, screaming, her dress splattered with blood.

"That five year-old girl's parents were killed by American forces when they mistakenly opened fired on her family's car as it approached a checkpoint in northern Iraq in January, 2005."

She turned back to face her audience.

"Today the Middle East is more violent and unstable than it has been in living memory – virtually all of that violence and instability a direct result of America's War on Terror. Iran and Saudi Arabia have entered into a proxy war of grave regional implications with no end in sight, the Saudis conducting a brutal, relentless dirty war in Yemen using child soldiers from Darfur in the front line, a war that's been supported by America from the get-go, countless of impoverished people dying from starvation as a result of the crisis. In the Middle East the United States is now in retreat, Russia and China asserting their power in the region, issuing open challenges to the world's former unipolar power. Europe is struggling from xenophobia born from a refugee crisis that has resulted directly from the violence of the wars in Afghanistan and Iraq, Britain and France in particular suffering a horrifying wave of terror attacks, events that would have been thought inconceivable prior to 9/11."

The image of the distraught five year-old Iraqi girl dissolved to a photo of unexploded mortars and bombs littering the streets of Mosul, dissolving to a photo of a member of the Syrian Civil Defense rescuing a wounded child from an aerial attack on Damascus by the Assad regime, then to the image of a young woman curled up in the fetal position on the grass in front of an American soldier's grave, a portrait of the young marine and the stars and stripes resting against the headstone. The screen went dark again a moment, the photo of a middle-aged Iraqi man and his son standing in the ruined yard their family home supplanting the photo of the young woman curled up on the grass in front of the marine's grave.

"That man is Ziad Abdul Qader. Beside him is his son Mohammad. They are standing in the courtyard of what was once their family home in Mosul. They fled the city when ISIS attacked. When they returned they found a dozen dead ISIS soldiers inside their ruined house. Today Mohammad suffers from panic attacks, and has forgotten how to read and write. The entire world has felt the devastating effects of the Iraq and Afghanistan Wars. After seventeen years of global chaos and instability, it's hard to characterize the invasions of these countries by America and the endless War on Terror as anything less than the original sin of the 21st century. Hence the title of this talk."

Julia paused a moment, then went on. "So who were/are the winners in Iraq?"

The image on the screen dissolved to a huge stash of bars of gold bullion surrounded by the logos of Boeing, Northrop Grumman, Lockheed Martin and Halliburton.

"Since the War on Terror was declared the annual salaries for CEOs of America's leading defense contractors has trebled to a combined total of over $1.5 billion, enough to cover the wages of three million Iraqis for a year. The wars in Iraq and Afghanistan have been a boom for the American arms industry, contracts for the top ten weapons contractors on average doubling, from $40 billion to $80 billion between 2001 and 2003, contracts held by Halliburton, Dick Cheney's alma mater as CEO, jumping more than nine times, from $400 million to $3.9 billion, Northrop Grumman's doubling, from $5.2 billion to $11.1 billion, and Lockheed Martin's, the largest U.S. arms company, seeing an increase of over 50%, from $14.7 billion to $21.9 billion."

The images dissolved to a blow up of Cheney, his twisted, cynical smile filling the screen.

"After Dick Cheney's tenure at the Pentagon ended in 1993, he spent the next years deciding whether or not to run for President. Forming a political-action committee, he crossed the country making speeches and raising money. Some of the biggest contributors to Cheney's PAC were not unsurprisingly leading executives of companies that won the largest contracts in Iraq -- Halliburton's CEO, Stephen Bechtel, whose family's firm won a contract worth $2.8 billion, and Duane Andrews, then senior VP of Science Applications International, a company awarded seven contracts in Iraq. But the biggest winner by far was Cheney's former company. In twelve months Halliburton went from being the Pentagon's thirty-seventh largest defense contractor with $500 million in contracts, to number seven, with $3.9 billion, later expanding to $8 billion in contracts for Iraqi rebuilding and Pentagon logistics work, finally hitting $18 billion once the company exercised all of its options. Halliburton's work included everything from rebuilding Iraq's oil infrastructure, to the construction of military bases, to providing meals for soldiers and maintaining military vehicles. Whenever and wherever the army had to deploy on short notice, Halliburton was there. Halliburton's bonanza from Iraq has been the gift that has kept on giving. It has never stopped. In January, 2017 it was announced the company signed a $210 million contract with Shell to drill thirty wells in Iraq's Majnoon oil field."

Julia turned and looked up at the screen again as the photo of Cheney dissolved to an image of George W. Bush, his brothers, Neil, Jeb, Marvin surrounding their father, George H.W. 'Poppy' Bush."

"When the Bush administration took office it appointed a total of thirty-two executives, paid consultants, or major shareholders of leading weapons contractors to top policymaking positions inside the Pentagon, the National Security Council, the Department of Energy, and the State Department. But it was the Bush family that amassed the largest fortune as a result of the Bush administration's exploitation of the courage of America's dead soldier heroes, the victims of 9/11 and the War on Terror."

She turned back to her audience, moving to her position front stage center again.

"I'm not going to bore you with the details of the myriad ways in which the Bush clan have profited from 9/11 and the War on Terror, including a lesser known family member, George W.'s uncle, William 'Bucky' Bush. Suffice it to say, dig deep enough and you'll find conclusive evidence of all of them getting fat and happy as a result of the events that followed 9/11 -- including the 'coincidence' that George H.W. Bush worked for the Bin Laden family business in Saudi Arabia, having persuaded the Rockefellers of the Middle East to invest money in a company in which Poppy Bush was a major shareholder, The Carlyle Group, one of the largest multinational private equity and alternative asset management corporations in the world. Carlyle owned and managed many companies that scored big-time in the Homeland Security bonanza of post 9/11 America, two of them, U.S. Investigations Services, and Federal Data Systems, earning multi-billion-dollar contracts with the government to provide background checks for the Pentagon, the CIA, and the Department of Homeland Security, both companies formerly Federal Agencies until they were privatized in 1996, and taken over by Carlyle."

The image of the Bush clan dissolved to the photo of the Twin Towers cascading to the ground.

"Nor am I going to give more than a passing mention to the other surreal 'coincidence' connecting the Bush family to 9/11 -- the fact that George W.'s youngest brother, Marvin Bush, was on the board of directors of the company that provided electronic security for the World Trade Center, United Airlines, the owner and operator of the plane that flew into the South Tower, and Dulles International Airport, from which the American Airlines plane which allegedly crashed into the Pentagon departed on the morning of

9/11."

The image of the Twin Towers dissolved to a photo of a terrified Iraqi family fleeing the chaos of Baghdad in the wake of the American invasion.

"Instead of wasting time detailing the obvious, I'm going to focus on the bigger picture, just like that family of men I have been speaking of for the past few minutes."

The photo of the family of Iraqi refugees dissolved to an image of George W. Bush, Cheney, Rumsfeld, and Paul Wolfowitz.

"You see, the men who have profited so obscenely from the War on Terror weren't content with simply securing billions of dollars from weapons, defense, construction and security contracts. They had their eyes on a much bigger, far more lucrative, long-term prize. No weapons of mass destruction were ever found in Iraq -- because they didn't exist. Bush, Cheney, Rumsfeld, Wolfowitz and their cronies in the *Project For A New American Century* knew it. Is it any wonder the entire population of Iraq, and so many of the American troops that served in the invasion and subsequent occupation of the country are asking 'Why did this happen?', 'Why was America ever there?'.

The image of Bush, Cheney, Rumsfeld and Wolfowitz dissolved to a photo of a towering jet back stream of oil gushing from a well in the desert as Julia read out a series of quotes.

"Of course it's about oil. We can't really deny that." General John Abizaid, former head of U.S. Central Command, Iraq. "I am saddened it is politically incorrect to acknowledge what everyone knows; the Iraq war is largely about oil." Alan Greenspan, former Chairman of the Federal Reserve. "People say we're not fighting for oil. Of course we are. They talk about America's national interest. What do hell do you think they're talking about? We're not there for figs." Chuck Hegal, Obama's Secretary of Defense

"Iraq is home to the world's second largest proven oil reserves, an estimated 112.5 billion barrels. Seventeen years since Operation Iraqi Freedom was launched, America bombing the hell out of Baghdad, while most of the American led coalition forces have long since departed, Western oil companies are barely getting started. Before the war, Iraq's oil industry was nationalized, closed to Western oil companies. Today it is largely privatized, dominated by foreign firms. From ExxonMobil and Chevron, to BP and Shell, the West's largest oil companies have set up shop, the majority serviced by American oil service companies, one of the biggest of which is Halliburton."

"An image of Bush, Cheney, Rumsfeld and Wolfowitz surrounded by a cluster of missiles, the words 'Blood For Oil. The Oiljackers; Armed With A Lot More Than Just Box-cutters' appeared on the screen.

"If the chilling, cold-blooded disdain of big oil for the endless pain, suffering and bloodshed that have resulted from the War on Terror was not crystal clear, the surreal truth would be almost laughable. As it is, the fact that the majority of the world refuses to look at, let alone acknowledge the truth and find the courage to bring to trial in an international court of law the heinous doings of those whom I am labelling in this talk 'Murder, Inc.' -- is tragic proof of the effectiveness of what I term in *Total War, Rampant Greed*, the mass propaganda and mind control practiced by these cold-hearted, despicable members of the human race."

The image of Bush, Cheney, Rumsfeld and Wolfowitz dissolved back to the photo of the Millennial in the skimpy bikini shooting a selfie.

"There is a reason why the narcissistic Millennial you see in the photo behind me, and millions like her, as well as her parents and grandparents can't be bothered, don't want to know, have no interest in addressing a truth that is too dark and too disturbing to acknowledge."

The photo of the Millennial morphed back to the 'Blood For Oil' image of Bush, Cheney, Rumsfeld and Wolfowitz.

"For the first time in thirty years, Western oil companies are exploring for and producing oil in Iraq, reaping enormous profits. This outcome was by design, the result of a decade of American government and oil company pressure prior to 9/11. In 1998, Kenneth Derr, then CEO of Chevron, said, 'Iraq possesses huge reserves of oil and gas -- reserves I'd love Chevron to have access to.' Today it does. In 2000, Big Oil, including Exxon, Chevron, BP and Shell, spent more money getting fellow oilmen Bush and Cheney elected than they had spent on any previous election. Just over a week into Bush's first term their efforts paid off when the National Energy Policy Development Group was formed, chaired by Cheney, bringing the big oil companies and the government together to plot their collective energy future. In March, 2000 the group reviewed lists and maps outlining Iraq's entire oil productive capacity, the planning for a military invasion soon under way. In 2004, Bush's first Treasury secretary, Paul O'Neill, stated publicly that already by February, 2001, seven months before 9/11, the talk was about logistics.

"Not the why to invade Iraq, but the when and the how, and how quickly.'"

Julia turned and looked up at the screen as the image dissolved back to the photo of Cheney, his foot propped up on his desk at the U.S. President's Emergency Operations Center watching news reports of the Twin Towers burning. The photo held a few moments, then morphed into the photo of a mangled, twisted, bloody human corpse, missing the lower portion of its body, spread-eagled on a street below the World Trade Center.

"They got what they wanted. This what was left of one of the jumpers on 9/11, the people trapped inside the Towers who plunged to their deaths rather than suffer a slow, torturous end being burnt to a cinder inside the buildings."

The image wiped to a shot of the jumpers leaping to their deaths from the South Tower, that image then morphing to a quote projected onto the screen, which Julia read aloud.

"All this was inspired by the principle -- which is quite true within itself -- that in the big lie there is always a certain force of credibility; because the broad masses of a nation are always more easily corrupted in the deeper strata of their emotional nature than consciously or voluntarily; and thus in the primitive simplicity of their minds they more readily fall victims to the big lie than the small lie, since they themselves often tell small lies in little matters but would be ashamed to resort to large-scale falsehoods."

Adolf Hitler, *Mein Kampf*

The screen went black.

"I haven't touched on the torture carried out by the CIA and American forces at Guantanamo Bay and Abu Ghraib prison in Iraq, without question the most abominable, unspeakable, shameful legacy of America's War on Terror. The monstrous, unforgivable, inhuman treatment of prisoners of war a memory that will never be forgotten -- a tragic stain on the identity of the American nation that will never disappear. As recent as eighteen months ago a United Nations human rights investigator reported that an inmate of the Guantanamo Bay detention facility was being tortured, despite Washington having banned American "enhanced interrogation techniques" a dozen years ago. Incredibly, Cheney was still defending his policy of wholesale, nefarious torture a few years ago on a chat show while promoting his miserable shell of an autobiography, *Exceptional*."

A quote from Cheney's book appeared on the screen. Again Julia read the quote aloud.

"Our children need to know that they are citizens of the most powerful, good and honorable nation in the history of mankind, the exceptional nation. We have guaranteed freedom, security, and peace for a larger share of humanity than has any other nation in all of history. There is no other like us. There never has been. We are, as a matter of empirical fact and undeniable history, the greatest force for good the world has ever known."

The quote dissolved back to the image of the Twin Towers crumbling to dust. Julia turned her back on her audience again, staring up at the screen.

"There is no other like us. There never has been." Those are the only truthful words in Cheney's entire hollow travesty of an autobiography."

She turned back for the final time her audience, reading aloud another quote from Hitler's *Mein Kampf* as it appeared on the screen

"For the grossly impudent lie always leaves traces behind it, even after it has been nailed down, a fact which is known to all expert liars in this world and to all who conspire together in the art of lying."

Adolf Hitler, *Mein Kampf*

Behind her on the screen Hitler's quote was replaced by a close up of the Statue of Liberty, Lady Liberty weeping, burying her head in her hands in shame.

"Ladies and gentlemen, I give you the United States of Infamy -- Murder, Inc."

ABOUT THE AUTHOR

A polymath Renaissance man in literature, the theater, film and television, Gregory Paul Martin has led a double life as a master astrologer his entire career. Trained as an actor at London's Royal Academy of Dramatic Art, his roles on stage including Hamlet, Peer Gynt, Edmund the Bastard in *King Lear*, and the world premieres of *Bent* in London and Harold Pinter's *One For The Road* at The Manhattan Theater Club in New York, in addition to *Watch It Come Down* in 2019 he will be publishing two novels — *Cabal*, a geopolitical thriller dealing with the monumental themes of human consciousness, corruption and power he writes about in this book, and *Redemption*, a thriller about the most deadly serial killer of all time.

The distillation of lifetimes as a master astrologer and seer of the highest degree going back to before the time of Christ, *Watch It Come Down* is a seminal work on the monumental revolution in human consciousness we are in the midst of today, its implications for mankind, and what Mr. Martin describes as the death and rebirth of America. A work of profound truth, wisdom and transformational power, *Watch It Come Down* explains in crystal clarity why America is going through a period of such tremendous turmoil, why Trump was elected President, and how to change your life during these troubled times so that you, your children, and the others you love begin to live on a future timeline of prosperity, power and peace.

Printed in Great Britain
by Amazon